T0209129

FREE SPIRIT

TRANSCENDING THE EGO

freeing yourself from that self-sabotaging inner voice
and making peace with your true spirit

TESSA SUTHERLAND

BALBOA
PRESS

A DIVISION OF HAY HOUSE

Balboa Press books may be ordered through booksellers or by contacting:

Balboa Press
A Division of Hay House
1663 Liberty Drive
Bloomington, IN 47403
www.balboapress.com.au
1 (877) 407-4847

Print information available on the last page.

ISBN: 978-1-5043-0315-6 (sc)
ISBN: 978-1-5043-0316-3 (e)

Balboa Press rev. date: 07/12/2016

Contents

Dedication

I dedicate this book to my two daughters in the hope that when they find life to be a struggle, they will find some solace within this book.

Introduction

Our existence on this earth is much more than this temporary physical state. We are all here for a unique purpose. We are all connected to the same source – divine intelligence. We all encounter challenging situations and bitter feelings, and we are all in search of this mysterious thing called happiness. The ego (fear) self that is within us all is what creates most of the pain and suffering that we experience in life. The ego is a limiting barrier that keeps us in a state of separateness – alone and divided from each other, our source and ourselves. Before we entered this physical realm we only knew happiness and love; thus, our quest to find and remember those qualities in this lifetime.

It is time to become conscious of the truth – that we are in control of our own lives. Our lives are based on our own perceptions of reality and when we realise that we have the power to change those perceptions to a different, more optimistic and liberated mindset, our lives will change accordingly.

Through love and spirit we can transcend the ego and experience an awakening of unlimited proportions. When we release ourselves from the confines of the ego we will maintain true meaning and a deep connection with the universe. We will know the truth – that everything happens for a reason. Our lives will begin to unfold in ways we could never imagine. We will begin to understand that we are more than just our physical bodies and that our consciousness survives death. We will discover our impersonal self on a spiritual journey towards awakening – the true essence of who we really are.

The flight of the eagle represents free spirit.

The eagle in all of its magnificence defies conformity and follows its own individual chosen calling. It is free from all concerns and obligations and trusts in the nature of spirit. It sees the beauty in the universe and represents freedom, strength, choice and independence.

The eagle accepts and honours the reason for creation, thus its intentions are spent in flight being free; free to choose, free to experience and free to just live and be whatever it chooses to be.

This is our quest for life. We just have to know it and allow it to be.

Transcending the ego – freeing yourself from that self-sabotaging inner voice and making peace with your true spirit.

Included are a collection of quotes from the Tao Te Ching – an incredible book written by Lao Tzu, a Chinese philosopher way back around 6th Century BC.

The words Tao Te Ching translate to "The book of the way and its power".

Lao Tzu translates to "Old Master".

Lao Tzu supposedly worked in the court of the Chou dynasty for most of his life, but eventually he grew tired of people who failed to take any notice of his ideas. In the face of relentless warfare, human suffering and an unresponsive government, he decided that he would leave human society and pursue a life of contemplation as a hermit in the wilderness. The gatekeeper however had always been deeply impressed with Lao Tzu's teachings. He refused to let Lao Tzu exit the court until he had written down his teachings. The legend has it that Lao Tzu sat down and wrote the Tao Te Ching in its entirety at one sitting, entrusted it to the gate-keeper and then left the state of Ch'u, never to appear in human society again.

The Tao Te Ching is considered to be one of the wisest books ever written. The Tao Te Ching presents an incredibly insightful philosophy which offers to us all new ways in which to incorporate love, peace and balance into our lives.

I have included these quotes, as what Lao Tzu is offering to us in his wisdom is the opportunity to change our way of thinking. His philosophy is that if we can change our thoughts we can change our lives and that to me has been the most powerful and intriguing lesson that I have learned in my life so far.

Chapter One
THE EGO

In the beginning

Before the universe began, we were all pure consciousness. We were all one with universal energy. We were all in spirit. We knew nothing of this physical realm, or our physical bodies with which we live today. We all co-existed as non-physical energy enclosed within the white light of unconditional love and contentment with no concept of time or space.

There was no meaning of hatred, fear, guilt or blame. There was just pure unconditional love and light. There was no meaning of darkness.

While we were in the dimension of spirit, all we knew was unconditional love, and with love came peace, joy, fulfilment, happiness and freedom.

Our spirits knew this eternal love conceptually and we took it for granted. We didn't know anything else. We didn't know how wonderful happiness was, because we had nothing to compare it to. Our spirit's desire was to seek to turn its concept about itself into experience. We wanted to know ourselves physically. Until we could turn concept into experience, we could only speculate on what love felt like.

Our spirits were created into a human form so that we could experience the magic of a lifetime in a physical body as opposed to only knowing ourselves as pure spirit. Physicality is the way to experience what we knew conceptually and this is the reason the universe was created.

The law of relativity which governs this universal state is that in order to be able to experience unconditional love, its opposite must be created: Fear. And so out of the lightness, darkness was created – a dichotomy by which many more would follow. A little darkness would help us see the light because then we would have something to compare it to.

That darkness that is applicable to everything that is associated with fear, we called ego.

Ego, the darkness, was introduced to us to help define love.

Just as fire was introduced to water, male was introduced to female and summer was introduced to winter.

The purpose of the theory of relativity is that we cannot know the experience of summer, without having had the experience of winter. We cannot know how hot feels, until we experience cold, and we cannot experience ourselves as what we are until we have experienced ourselves as what we are not. It is by that which we are not, that we are characterised.

A dichotomy is an illusion. Anything that did not come from spirit is an illusion. Fear, blame, hurt, guilt, unworthiness, doubt, shame, anger and hate are all illusions – created so that we may become aware of everything that was born in spirit – love, peace, happiness, joy, pleasure and harmony.

Fear is false evidence appearing real.

Everything that we experience in this lifetime will be a result of our decision to operate out of LOVE or FEAR. There are only ever two choices.

Upon entering this physical universe we were required to relinquish our memories of our lifetimes in the spirit world. When we surrendered our memory of this we forgot who we were, thus allowing free will to be put into place which gave us the choice of who we wanted to be and what experience we wanted to create.

When we arrived into this realm we were the perfect example of unconditional love – because that is what we came from.

And so it was – 15 billion years ago – time began and we took on a physical form and ego was created.

Most people associate with "that little voice inside their head". In fact there are two voices but most people can only hear the ego's dominant voice. The ego is the false self, created from fear. Spirit is the true self – or the sacred self, created from unconditional love.

The ego's voice continually speculates, judges, shames and compares our lives with those of others. It imagines the outcome of any possible situation to be disastrous and continually exploits us with negative messages about our self worth. It is that critical internal monologue that reminds us of our weaknesses and failings. Some of us can spend a whole lifetime struggling with who we think we are by being constantly instructed by the ego's narcissistic voice. We let fear (ego) dominate our lives, and then we berate ourselves for failing to achieve success. We deem ourselves unworthy.

The ego's voice is a mirror that reflects back to us who we think we are. It over-rides our inherent intelligence and concept of reality by superimposing its beliefs about what is real. It has a delusional image of life that distorts reality.

The ego is the thinking part of the mind that reacts to reality and has given us a sense of our own identity, individuality and self esteem.

Our ego defines itself by relating to the people, ideas and objects around it. This process is continuous. Our identity must be continuously reinforced or we will quite literally lose the sense of who we are.

The ego drives us to make decisions that always place us in a position of being hurt. The ego is a false self and is at the cause of all of our delusions and suffering.

The ego's voice denies us feeling worthy, adequate or loved and the ego is always a victim of circumstance – the belief that "I'm not good enough" is the ego's main addiction. The ego's voice takes over our joy by filling us with pain, worries, concerns, regrets and shame.

For example:
"You are not good enough".
"You never get it right".
"You are not pretty enough".
"You don't do enough".

"Nobody likes you".
"You're going to make a fool of yourself".
"Don't bother trying – you know you can't do it".

The ego is a way of relating to the world our beliefs about ourselves from what we have learned. The ego comes from a state of being socially conditioned, with certain programmes installed into us based on life experiences.

It is formed by a collection of memories and bad experiences, negative childhood beliefs and criticisms from our earliest teachers. The ego is generated on the basis of past events or circumstances. These beliefs were imprinted onto our minds before our logical thinking mind had a chance to develop enough so that we could filter through these messages.

The ego begins to enforce its existence at an early age. Up until this point spirit had operated predominately because we were new and freshly arrived from a reality of pure love and light. Infants and toddlers often arrive here with the memories of their lifetimes in the dimension of spirit and often claim to "start to forget" at about four or five years of age. We were living unconditional love up to that point because that is what we came from therefore all that we knew. As we grow, we gradually lose our intimate knowledge of the spirit world. Memory resides at the level of the soul until we can recall it.

Our birth is but a sleep and a forgetting:
The soul that rises with us, our life's star
Hath had elsewhere its setting,
And cometh from afar:
Not in entire forgetfulness,
And not in utter nakedness,
But trailing clouds of glory do we come
From God, who is our home:
Heaven lies about us in our infancy!
Shades of the prison-house begin to close
Upon the growing Boy,
But he beholds the light, and whence it flows,
He sees it in his joy;

> The youth, who daily farther from the east
> Must travel, still is Nature's priest,
> And by the vision splendid
> Is on his way intended;
> At length the Man perceives it die away,
> And fade into the light of common day.
> A verse from Intimations of Immortality
> William Wordsworth

It is at this stage in our childhood when our consciousness has evolved enough so that we are able to come to the conclusion that we are separate from our source. This is the foundation of the ego.

Gradually, as we began to separate ourselves from the spirit world the ego expanded. Eventually we separated ourselves from nature, from each other and from ourselves. The resulting feelings of separateness led to anxiety and pain. The light in our hearts became clouded by fear and began to fade from our awareness. The ego slowly began to take over our lives.

As children we cope with separation by allowing the ego to deal with the world. This allows two destructive core beliefs to develop:

1. The world is a dangerous place (fear).
2. I am unworthy (shame).

The ego becomes fixated at the level of the child and is unable to mature. Life then becomes a constant struggle to feel safe, secure and worthy.

In our childhood stages we take in the personalities, points of view, opinions, morality and belief structures of those closest to us and we incorporate them into our own character structure. They become part of our internal world. Our self image is formed by the appraisals and criticisms of others. We internalise the way those close to us interpret us and that becomes incorporated into how we see ourselves. Interpretation happens at the level of the mind, but it is our individual ego that is conditioned by experience; and through that memory of past experiences the ego influences our choices and interpretations in life. It forms an imprint of the way we see ourselves and that in turn impacts on the creation of ourselves. Fundamentally, it forms the foundation of who we think we are. The belief system of who we think we are is then recorded into our minds and continues to be as we move through life. It has everything to do with defining who we are. We therefore create our own lives through our own thoughts and beliefs that we hold as true.

Fear of abandonment is the first of many fears which begin when the child realises that it is an individual and separate from its mother. With this realisation comes the fact that as an individual it is totally helpless, dependent and at the mercy of its parents for all forms of sustenance, means of survival and love. To a child abandonment by its parents is the equivalent of death.

As a child abandonment can be perceived in many different ways – death, negligence, divorce, lack of time or lack of love.

As time goes on the child realises with dismay that in order to have its parents' approval and love, it is not enough to merely be itself. We have to act in accordance with certain rules and regulations, and certain demands of life. We realise then that we are not loved unconditionally, but conditionally, and we arrive at the assumption that somehow there is something about us that is incomplete; that we were somehow not good enough. This creates a hurt, lost, frightened and angry child and once this image becomes ingrained in our minds, it alters our perception of ourselves and thus becomes a firm belief in our core being. A child perceives a lack of love as a threat to its survival.

The strength of our ego will depend on our childhood conditioning. If we grew up believing that we were valued, worthy and loved unconditionally, our egos would not be the source of our pain. Anyone who has had a childhood full of love, will know at his core that he is valued. This is the most precious gift that anyone can give to a child. A feeling of being valued is essential to mental health and if not gained in childhood, is extremely difficult to acquire in adulthood. If a child is valued from childhood, it sets them up with a strong spirit that cannot be destroyed by the often destructive circumstances of adult life.

If, however, we grew up believing that we were unworthy or unloved, we will have gone through life attracting everything that supported that belief system. If we feel that we have no value we will grow up feeling unworthy and therefore we won't necessarily take care of ourselves. This often leads to self destructive behaviours and addictions.

The love and quality of the time that a parent devotes to the child, indicates to the child the degree to which they are valued by the parent.

Since children do not have the benefit of comparison, we look at our parents as God-like figures. Because they are adults, our role models and our carers, we take for granted that what they do or say is the right way and so when love is absent, it teaches the child that they are unworthy of love. The child then grows up with the impression that they are not good enough, thus spend the rest of their lives trying to seek validation and love from their parents and the rest of the world.

If we felt that we were unworthy and not valued as a child, our egos would tell us that even as adults we needed to continually seek out other's love or approval in order to feel validated or worthy.

Ego still threatens us today with the fear of being unsafe if we are not loved.

Thus our search for unconditional love and approval then becomes a life long journey. Our lives begin with a search in vain for validity.

Even as adults we maintain the defence mechanisms that were appropriate in our early childhood. We live through the eyes of those helpless little children that can be so easily hurt through the traumatising events of our childhood, neglecting the fact that as adults we are much more able to tolerate.

Very often therefore the critical inner voice is that of a young child – a wounded child.

When we grow up with the belief that somehow we are unworthy or unlovable, our lives will reflect that belief. Those false concepts will have manifested themselves inside our consciousness. Our ego's acceptance of the concept that we are unworthy is apparent by its tendency to seek love and acceptance from the outside as opposed to the inside.

We measure our worth and entitlement to love by our capacity to win approval.

The ego continually seeks approval and validation on the external level. We learn at a young age most of our life's lessons through the approval or disapproval of our parents. Because the need for approval is so strong, we become conditioned over time to seek validation from others. This means feeling loved and accepted, safe and protected. Whenever there is a situation where we do not receive approval, there is an automatic response to win that approval. When we are met with disapproval we undermine the view we have of ourselves. We will internalise the negative feedback and that in turn causes us to doubt our personal worth. This threatens our sense of security and paves the way for a lifetime belief of "I am unworthy".

Seeking love through our egos, from the outside in, will never succeed because our egos are not our true being and we will never find adequate self-love through gaining approval from others. We can only find it by a deep appreciation and a love for ourselves that goes beneath the shallow confines of the ego. We need to go within and realise that we are all divine spirit.

The unconscious drive behind the ego is ultimately to shield us from spirit; thus strengthening the image of who it thinks it is by being in total control, demanding more power and striving for more attention. Ego has a total sense of separation and the need for opposition. It has a sense of insufficiency and lack that continuously needs to be filled and is never satisfied with any outcome we may arrive at. When we are operating out of ego, we are always operating out of fear.

Whoever can see through all fear will always be safe.

Lao Tzu

Happiness is the source that we all know and try so hard to attain, because we have known it so well. The feeling of deep contentment and intense joy are an innate desire of human beings. We strive for our purpose, but the darkness conceals it. Ego is the dark shadow, immobilising us, guarding us from reaching the light.

Enlightenment is what we all yearn for, but by allowing ourselves to be manipulated by the fears that the ego creates, we keep destiny just out of our reach.

The ego holds many illusions:

Approval through possessions

Somehow, down through the centuries, society has adopted the wrong interpretation of our purpose in life. We have somehow come to the conclusion that to be successful in life is to conform to society's expectation of material wealth. The ego identifies with money, possessions and social status. Success from this perspective is defined by that which is superficially centred on the external. We are fulfilling our purpose by a completely materialistic viewpoint and it is a direction that has completely sabotaged our spirituality.

It is the ego's compulsion to enhance our identity through associating with material possessions. The ego is based on a selfish desire for ambition and more possessions and the power that it derives from acquiring these. Ego identifies with possessions that fill up the emptiness inside ourselves and creates attachment to them which in turn creates the ego's mantra of "more". Then a preoccupation with material possessions becomes apparent. The ego continues to fill up our lives with possessions in order to increase our sense of self worth.

The ego informs us that the world is based on an external focus, thus the material world is our only reality. This in turn leaves us with an emptiness – we feel incomplete; that there is something missing from our lives. We feel dissatisfied and unfulfilled, alone and lost. We lose touch with who we are and let our possessions define us. We lose touch with our inner self – our spirit. Ego lives in fear: Fear of not being good enough, and not having enough.

And so in order to fill that void we accumulate possessions, seek power, fame and wealth.

The ego's predominant voice is "more" or "how much can I acquire".

The ego is never satisfied in spite of its possessions, so it seeks to fortify itself through further acquisitions; we buy bigger houses and cars, get better jobs, and acquire more money. The more we have, the happier we think we will be. Whatever the ego seeks and acquires from the outside world are masks to cover the inner spirit.

Our ego's mission is to seek out validation, approval and admiration. We continuously look for new ways of trying to be worthy and possessions and achievements are all recruited into the game of validation.

Most of our conscious lifetime is spent trying to seek fulfilment on an external level instead of looking inward, and then we wonder why happiness and contentment are still so far out of our reach.

> If your happiness depends on money, you will never be happy with yourself.
>
> Lao Tzu

Approval through achievements

In order to obtain happiness, the ego thinks that we must achieve. The more achievements and the better skills we have, the more value we place on ourselves. We base our worthiness on our performance – the greater the achievement, the grander the human being we become. When we do not perform well we deem ourselves unworthy. Therefore the ego is always driving us to achieve bigger and greater things in order to validate ourselves. The ego tells us that we are all incomplete; there is something missing. The fear of exposing that emptiness drives us to fill that emptiness with achievements. We create a false image of contentment through the need to be ambitious – we feel the need to prove to everybody what a tremendously successful person we are. We must fight our way to the top of the ladder – outdo each other achieving, in order not to be left at the bottom. A hectic schedule and endless demands on our time affirms to the ego that we are important and needed and as a result our world has become rushed and fearful.

Ego relates to "survival of the fittest," "victory of the strongest," and "success of the cleverest".

Arrogance

Ego tell us that we have to be right. The ego needs to feel superior. To be wrong is to feel inferior as a human being. The moment anybody questions the ego's sacred beliefs the ego will become defensive.

When the ego's belief system is threatened, it becomes very defensive. The ego will dissociate with anybody who opposes their belief system. It will negate them, prove them wrong, and ignore them, all in order to protect what it believes to be true. The ego would rather be right than be free.

The ego perceives threatening events or feelings as attacks and the ego defends itself. Being defensive is the ego's primary activity.

The ego defends itself any time that it feels that its actions are being compromised. Defensiveness always stems from fear and guilt and the ego feels threatened, therefore feels that by attacking somebody else, can demonstrate its own power at the expense of another's vulnerability. Defensiveness creates conflict and so the cycle continues.

Complaining and finding fault in others is the ego's way of making somebody else at fault. The ego will find fault in anything and anybody to strengthen its sense of superiority. The ego has to be right and will argue its correctness.

This sense of "I am right" and "you are wrong" is essentially the underlying attitude of the ego. Therefore the ego is its own victim.

By making ourselves right and somebody else wrong we perpetuate separation and conflict between ourselves. When we have an attitude of "us" versus "them" we create a division between ourselves. This in turn creates greed, selfishness, exploitation and violence.

Distrust

The ego has a profound distrust towards everybody and everything in the world.

The ego does not trust in the process of life because it is skeptical of everything life has to offer. It doesn't take any responsibility for our lives because it doesn't think that we have any power to change the outcome of our lives. We live in a moment-by-moment attitude, just accepting these experiences and situations that randomly appear in our lives. We label ourselves victims of circumstance claiming that life is just happening to us. We must therefore endure all the unfortunate and unpleasant experiences because we cannot conceive of, much less believe that we as human beings are capable of changing our own lives.

We label these situations or experiences as coincidences, fate, chance or lucky and unlucky with no knowledge of the fact that the consequences of our lives are the result of the thoughts and decisions that we have made. Ego chooses to remain trapped within its own self sabotaging truth, thus holding us in situations which are completely inappropriate.

Ego insists that the world is an unfair, unpredictable place and that every person is only interested in pleasing and providing for themselves. It is the human beings that apply the ultimate betrayals, therefore to open themselves up to the world would be deemed somewhat preposterous and illogical to the ego's operating mind. Ego's doubts, worries, insecurities and fears then take over which prevent us from discovering the joy in our lives.

The ego believes that there is a limited amount of life's necessities, which creates greed and competitiveness and so we find the need to fight among ourselves to get our fair share. The resulting conclusion is therefore the need to protect the things closest to us – ourselves, our family and our possessions.

We feel the need to enforce defence strategies against those who hurt, manipulate, cheat and steal from us. Those defensive strategies involve rules and regulations, rewards and punishments, jail and death sentences.

As a result ego or fear (of which distrust is a component) is the leading cause of all the theft, war, crime, bullying, addictions, transgressions or misconduct that happens in the world.

At its best the ego is suspicious, at its worst the ego is vicious.

> The more laws and order are made prominent, the more thieves and robbers there will be.
>
> Lao Tzu

Approval through reputation

Ego tells us that we have to be tremendously dependent on what other people think of us. We become so immersed in serving our own egos that other people's opinions have become more important to us than our own. We have become so devoted to pleasing other people that we make ourselves out to be something other than what we are – all in the hope of impressing somebody else or to win other people's approval. Our mental concept of ourselves is rated according to the approval, respect or trust that we receive from others. Many of us act as if doing all the things that society tells us we should be doing will eventually bring us success and happiness.

Caring about what other people think constitutes every aspect of ego's life. We define ourselves by our popularity and the way that other people view us: Whether it be caring about our physical appearance, making certain life choices, or choosing which possession will make us look more superior. The ego craves attention and we feel the need for others to see us in a certain perspective. The ego requires approval from others and as long as we have their approval, we have permission to put ego at rest. When we feel that we are not recognised or acknowledged by others, our ego automatically comes to the conclusion that we are inadequate or unloved.

The proven method of measuring our success is by comparing ourselves with those around us. The ego is always telling us that we are "not good enough" so it is always at work trying to improve itself so that we will be acceptable to the outside world. The ego is continuously moulding itself towards likeability and so we tiptoe through life, carefully manoeuvring our way around different people and different experiences using only the strategies we think are required for those certain tasks. The price that we pay is that we are constantly being manipulated and shaped into something that we are not. We allow others to control the person we are. We take on other people's beliefs and opinions, values and expectations. We suppress our own emotions and desires in an attempt to conform to society's beliefs of what is acceptable. When we seek approval from others we are not being true to ourselves. We define ourselves as "good" or "bad" or "fat" or "thin" and that throws us into conflict. We lead ourselves into a battle of good and evil and we continually have to live up to other's expectations. In doing so we set ourselves up for constant pain and suffering. What people think about us is not important. What we think about ourselves means everything.

> Care about what other people think and you will always
> be their prisoner.
>
> Lao Tzu

Approval through appearance

Ego insists that our identity is completely determined by our appearance. It seeks validation externally. Ego derives our identity with our physical appearance. It wants to keep us stuck in the illusion that the body is a separate entity – the body is all that there is – therefore all that we are. The ego tells us to look for the inside on the outside. The outer illusion is the major preoccupation of the ego. It persuades us that what we see with our sense of sight is in fact our reality. Our body is the most visible and palpable expression of who we are, thus the easiest target for the attacks of the ego.

We have come to believe that we are what we look like, and so how we appear to the outside world becomes the most influential factor in our everyday lives. We live in a culture that is obsessed with external validation. We try to cultivate our image to impress as many people as possible. We carefully curate our lives in order to seem as impressive as possible, wanting confirmation that we are adequate, worthy and loveable.

Our egos have created an illusion where the world has an expectation of what we should look like, and if we don't conform to those images we are deemed inferior. We rate our value on the approval of others and we are so concerned with our physical appearance that we neglect the internal spiritual self. We use our physical bodies as a canvas on which we paint a picture of ourselves to portray to the world what we want the world to think about us. We constantly compare and judge our bodies with others, and judge ourselves on our ability to adapt our personality or appearance to whatever society's definition of what is beautiful at that particular time. In a world dominated by the superficial the ego seeks comfort in status and recognition. Our sense of self is determined by our external appearance and many of us feel a diminished sense of self worth when we conceive of ourselves to be something other than what is deemed by society's expectations as acceptable. Ultimately we wind up not knowing who we are as we become so absorbed in conforming to the concepts of what we think we should be, in order to seek approval. By relying on external validation we are inherently surrendering our identity and self worth to others.

There is absolutely no happiness to be found in a materialistic environment. When our lives are dedicated to appearance, material gain, status and greed, there is no opportunity for spiritual growth and that will inevitably leave us feeling empty and miserable. To live a life dedicated to the ego is to live in hell.

The ego is profoundly an identification with the physical and material form, which results in an unawareness of our unity with each other and our connection to source. When we realise that all material possessions are impermanent we will awaken to the inner beauty and wisdom that resides within us all and is the only source of happiness and fulfilment.

The illusion of limitation

The ego constantly controls our thoughts by telling us that we are limited. We are confined within the five physical senses that we have been taught and that impacts on everything that we can do and say. In physical reality we tend to measure, count, contain and limit ourselves, our time and our resources. According to the ego, there is nothing beyond the five senses, hence we believe that there is nothing that we cannot see, hear, touch, feel and taste. We develop the perception that there are limitations and separations because the ego needs to make sense of the world. We need to enforce rules and regulations in order to overcome our fear of the unknown. We feel powerless without boundaries. We believe that we have limitations because that is true in the physical world.

The ego believes that there is nothing beyond the physical body and that life is purely a biological process. The ego believes that we are only here for a limited amount of time and when we die that is the complete end of our existence.

We believe that we are powerless to change or influence any external situation or experience and that the things that happen to us are purely random occurrences, therefore unexplained coincidences occur for no apparent reason.

The ego blames everybody and everything around it for the circumstances of our lives and the things that happen to us. We take on a victim perspective and wonder why the world is so incredibly unjust. There is absolutely no meaning or purpose to life and we conclude that life is more of a hardship, therefore we take on an overall negative perspective. The world seems to be inundated with difficulties and problems and we hold up our hands in dread and despair. Ego has at this point drowned out any potential sign of spirit beneath a huge pile of pain, suffering and wounds. Ego is so lost and confused amidst its suffering that there is no chance of spirit surfacing. The ego's self limiting beliefs are being lived in reality because the ego chose to establish and nurture those negative thoughts a long time ago. Therefore the content of our lives was defined way back then, before our rational thinking mind had a chance to develop, thus the consequences that we have received in life have remained unchanged.

We have no concept that we are capable of changing our thoughts, therefore changing our lives. The ego's attitude is that our thoughts are in control of us instead of us being in control of our thoughts.

The ego has an agenda that keeps us limited in our thoughts and abilities.

It cannot accept rejection, therefore it is afraid that if we experiment with new challenges and risk new experiences, we will ultimately fail and others will judge us on our imperfect attempts, so we remain cautious, remaining in the ever mundane patterns of life that we have created for ourselves. The ego lives in constant fear of the world and everything in it. To the ego the world is an unsafe and unpredictable place and it does not want to expose itself to the world for fear of rejection.

The illusion of time

The ego is always associated with guilt over the past or worry over the future. Ego cannot be found in the now, which is where we spend the least amount of our time. Ego destroys the present moment. Ego uses resistance as a tool by which to divert its energy.

Resistance is a conditioned response of the ego. It is the ego's effort to maintain control of the situation. The ego's resistance is based on fear of the unknown. The present moment contains the voice of intuition or spirit; therefore the ego blocks out our intuition by being completely preoccupied with guilt over the past or worry over the future. This is why it seems so difficult to stay focused in the present moment. One of ego's greatest illusions is the belief that the past is responsible for the current conditions of our lives.

Resistance brings us no peace – instead causes a rift inside of us, which causes tension in the body.

The illusion of separation

The illusion of separation demonstrated through thoughts, feelings and actions is the most detrimental obstacle to human growth. It is the fundamental cause of the sense of separation from all of life, and by far the most damaging deception to the fate of human consciousness.

Ego tells us that we are separate from all things: Separate from others, separate from the world, separate from spirit, separate from the universe, separate from love and mostly separate from ourselves. Ego considers itself to be separate from all things due to identification with the physical body. The illusion of separation is created by identifying too powerfully with the external. Ego thinks in terms of the five senses and has no ability to diversify beyond these beliefs. Ego thinks that the physical world of the senses where we feel pain and illness is the only reality. The ego thinks that this human existence is the only existence that we will ever have therefore has created an enormous fear based around death – death being the end of consciousness. Ego does not know about the larger reality – the realm of spirit.

Convinced of our separateness, ego views life as a competition. To help make the world a less frightening and unpredictable place our egos have invented rules and regulations, religions and laws to protect itself. Our sense of solitude drives us to seek outer connections. Because we are unable to see ourselves as connected to the whole invisible intelligence, we feel the need to prove ourselves better than others. We feel the need to look better, achieve more, accumulate more, judge, criticise others and find fault. We feel the need to fight for what we want and defeat our fellow man. Because we believe that we are disconnected and separate, we substitute outer connections for inner connections. We have come to believe that the physical life is all there is.

The ego corresponds with the power of "mine" as opposed to "ours". It thinks that we are all in it for ourselves; it is the "survival of the fittest".

It says, "I am in this alone – therefore I must fend for myself". The ego has no sense of unity or connection to others. Ego says, "I am in competition with the world – I am in this for myself – there is never enough, therefore I need to obtain as much as I can before somebody else takes it away from me". It is always looking out for its own selfish self.

Ego has taken over and abandoned the spirit world, leaving us feeling anxious, disconnected and lonely.

There is a deep and imperative need within the human ego to seek love and acceptance from other egos. This cannot take place where any shadows of hate, jealousy, anger or fear are present. Hate, jealousy, anger and fear are all negative attitudes that create a crevice between oneself and the rest of life.

The concept of our being separate from everybody else has led to fear and fear has led us to suffering, exploitation and abuse. Having lost touch with our inner wisdom, we turned outside ourselves for guidance, comfort and security. That is at the root of our global crises – war, torture, genocide, abuse and cruelty. It can be responsible for all of our mental illness including addiction, anxiety, depression and suicide. It has led to people trying to control the world and therefore the world is no longer a paradise; it is now seen as unfriendly and unsafe. The ego's attitude is that life is to be endured rather that enjoyed and fear seems to have become dominant in our lives.

The belief in separateness is the core messages of our early patriarchal religions such as Judaism and Christianity. "God" – who once had been known to be everywhere and everything all of the time, was redefined as a separate entity. "God" became a masculine "father figure" in the sky who sat in judgment of us, and could be so cruel and hateful that he would deem us to eternity in hell if we ate meat on a Friday or harboured a sinful thought, but if we were good, we would be rewarded in the afterlife. We were promised conditional love by a "mystical God," but only if we were good or perfect in return. This cosmology is based upon judgment and conditional love. This in itself destroys inner peace and self worth.

Life then becomes a battle between good and evil. And if we win the battle, if we are "good enough" we will win the approval of a God that is so conditional that He loves us only when we conform to his standards of behaviour.

> First God created us and then we created God.
> Marcus Borg and Ross Mackenzie: God at 2000

Religion is a belief in God – spirituality is a knowing. Spirituality is a knowing that we are all one. We all come from the divine universal source, therefore we are all a part of God.

Religion is a man-made concept of God and has so many negative connotations we would be wise to throw out this concept of God altogether.

Hell does not exist except that of a super imposed separation from our source.

Love is the one positive attitude that can heal the crevice.

When the ego (the illusion of separateness), underlies and governs how we live our lives, we will continue to live in a world full of fear, injustice, dysfunction, greed and the need for power. If the composition of the human mind remains unchanged we will continue to create a completely dysfunctional life experience for ourselves.

> The problem is that we have allowed our egos, the part
> of us which believes that we are separate from God and
> separate from each other, to dominate our lives.
> Wayne Dyer

The illusion of judgment

The ego cannot survive without judgment. Ego is always judging, blaming or finding fault in us.

Some common characteristics of the ego:

It tells us that unless we are a certain
way, nobody will like us.
It call us names: Fat, ugly, stupid, weak,
unworthy, etc and we believe it.
It creates rules and regulations defining
how we should behave.
It tells us we are to blame when things go wrong.
It tells us that when others are upset it is our fault.
It compares us to others and tells us
we will never be good enough.
It constantly reminds us that we are a failure.

The ego is judging and undermining us everyday of our lives. We are never good enough, we never quite stack up in the mind of the ego. There is always something that we need to prove. Ego's voice is so perpetual that we take it for granted and believe it to be the truth. We don't realise the devastating effects it has on our lives.

The ego judges others when we are jealous of them. They may have some possession, status or appearance that we would rather have for ourselves, because without it, the ego feels inferior to them.

The ego continually compares itself with others, and if somebody else is more intelligent or more articulate than we are, the ego instantly feels threatened so tries to restore its value by degrading or criticising that person in order to redeem itself. When we compete with others, the ego is merely trying to prove that it is better than the other and the ego always judges on the value of material objects.

The ego gossips so that it can temporarily boost its own superiority – its central message being "I am better than them". And in order to cling to that illusion, the ego justifies lying and cheating. And to further compensate, the ego encourages us to steal from, injure and kill our fellow men.

These immoral obligations we carry through relentlessly– anything to satisfy the selfish demands of the ego.

When we label and judge others, our own lives become shallow and meaningless.

When ego is in control of us, it is impossible to feel love or compassion in our minds, therefore ego inhibits our growth and development toward spirituality.

Forgiveness

Forgiveness is impossible for the ego.

The ego is incapable of love. Because it cannot love, it cannot forgive – which is the basis of compassion. The antonym of forgiveness is blame and the ego seeks justice and punishment so we carry around hurt, anger and resentment toward those people who caused us pain.

The ego demands that we refuse forgiveness because it gives us a sense of "power" and "control" over those who hurt us. By refusing forgiveness we forever hold a condemning inescapable guilt over them.

When ego refuses to forgive that which has occurred, it chooses to stay in the feud, the resentment and the feelings of angst.

We label ourselves as "victims" and take on the "poor me" attitude. As victims we live in the past, blaming past situations for the current state of our lives. "If only" becomes a well used phrase. Whenever we blame luck, fate, coincidence, heredity, childhood or parents, society or anybody for anything that happens in our lives we are in the victim mentality. We express our anger by destroying our own lives and thereby hurting others. We don't even consider the possibility that we create our own reality – instead we believe that life is just a random and meaningless exercise to be endured rather than enjoyed. We feel cheated of life as though we have been unfairly treated and we are constantly afraid, misunderstood and resentful. Victims feel a sense of being burdened by unattainable demands. We feel that we have no clear answers to life's problems and in that sense we feel utterly unworthy and hopeless.

Being a helpless victim of circumstance allows us to avoid taking responsibility for our own lives, to live with self pity rather than taking responsibility for ourselves and to punish others. Victims will always create disaster. Because they keep repeating the same old pattern without taking responsibility for themselves or their lives, they will endure trauma after trauma.

The ego is an expert at being defensive, at rationalising and justifying its own behaviour, at seeing itself as the victim of a harsh and cruel world. Ego takes pleasure in wallowing in self pity and defending itself at all costs. It is dishonest and manipulative. Blaming others and opting out of responsibility are two of the ego's most distinguishing characteristics.

The ego wants suffering and revenge and this requires a lot of negative thinking. Ego needs to learn that we create our own reality and that when we blame others we give away our power. While we believe that a problem is somebody else's fault, we cannot resolve it because we cannot change other people; we can only change ourselves. As we accept more responsibility we will enrich and empower our own lives. The more responsibility we take over our own lives the more we are able to create a life of happiness, joy and love.

Emotions are vibrating energy and when we hold onto negative energy it gets trapped in the body and disrupts the normal energy field of the body. These negative energy blocks are usually created from resentment and anger and they eat away at the body and can cause cancer.

The greatest freedom is to be responsible.

Lazaris

Gratitude

The opposite of gratitude is criticism. The ego thrives on dissatisfaction.

The ego does not realise the gift of life and therefore feels a sense of entitlement for anything and everything in this universe. The ego thinks that the world revolves around it. It actually cultivates a sense of entitlement for itself which conflicts with the growth of spirit. The more we feel entitlement, the less ability we have to feel gratitude.

The ego will rarely put others people's needs before its own, and it is difficult for ego to comprehend the idea that it has benefited in numerous ways because of the efforts and sacrifices of other people. The ego continuously takes everything for granted without seeing the beauty in any shape or form.

The ego will often take on a victim attitude – "The poor me attitude" – and proclaim that the world is unfair or unjust because there are so many deficiencies in the world, and it is always demanding more.

Self absorption comes in many forms: Guilt, entitlement, manipulating others, being unable to apologise, inability to let go of anger, fears, worries and anxiety are a few.

All of these ego attitudes sabotage our potential to feel grateful, and to be grateful is what gives life its meaning. Gratitude requires an open heart and a clearing of the mind which will create space for gratitude to reside.

Most people don't challenge or question the ego's voice and instead take it for granted, listen and follow its negative orders without any doubt, accepting that reaction as just the way it is. We believe our ego to be our main identity. And so we stay stuck in the cycle of anger, hatred and hurt – classic expressions of the ego. In doing so we give the ego permission to stay in control of our lives.

> To serve your ego is to worship a false identity created by yourself. It's like someone who is suffering from amnesia reinventing herself because she has forgotten who she is.
> (The Tao is Tao, 80)

Luckily when we were created, we were given free will – and that means that we have free will to resist the ego. We can correct the illusion of fear and all of its dependents by bringing spirit to ourselves. It is our choice as to whether we would rather be a hostage to ego or a host to spirit.

The divisions, prejudices and illusions that we perceive in this world today are purely ego created. These qualities are not the result of spirit turning away from us but in this ego dominated world it is of us turning away from spirit.

The ego is a terrible task master who drives you to distress
Once your spirit is exhausted you will be irretrievably lost
The Taoist sage has no ego driving her to exhaustion
She is never too busy for she does
not flee from her true self.

Tao Te Ching

Chapter two
SPIRIT

There are two halves of us: The spirit and the ego. When we are in ego, we are operating out of fear. The outcomes of fear are the feelings of hurt, insecurity, being judged, unworthiness, hatred, bitterness, anger, sadness, jealousy, loneliness, selfishness, blame, guilt, dishonesty, violence, resentment, fear, worry and anxiety.

There is no illusion greater than fear.

Lao Tzu

When we are operating out of spirit, we are operating out of unconditional love. Spirit feels love no matter what the condition of our life.

When we are in spirit we will feel love, contentment, joy, blessed, happy, fulfilled, grateful and peaceful.

Feeling like this is the yearning that we have not been able to identify, but have always known to be true. This is the purpose of life itself. We are continually seeking to find how we felt BEFORE we separated from spirit. Being joyful is our natural state of being, thus our eternal quest for peace and happiness.

Love is the most powerful emotion on earth. Love has the ability to heal all things. Love is a choice which creates options. Ego is a choice but it removes options. True love is recognising that love is a gift which becomes perfect when it is unconditionally given and unconditionally received. It is the faith, the assurance, the confidence, the belief that we are all loved and that love is given freely. The acceptance depends on us. Whether we accept the love or reject it all depends on faith. Love is more that an emotion. Love is a choice.

There are really only two emotions in the physical universe – those being love and fear. All other emotions are just variations on these two primary states of emotion. Love is the emotion associated with the knowledge that everything in the universe is an expression of spirit and is therefore interconnected, whereas fear is the illusion of being separate from spirit.

Love is an expression of the oneness that underlies all reality associated with a deeply felt knowing that everything is an expression of source and that nothing (no-thing) can exist outside source. By contrast, fear is rooted in the illusory perception of separation that pervades the physical universe.

Love expresses itself as an urge towards unity, whereas fear is a result of the perception of dis-unity that is part and parcel of ego's game of separation that defines the physical universe. (i.e. The "them" versus "me" syndrome associated with the isolation currently experienced by most humans.)

Love is a state of "knowing," whereas fear is based entirely upon "beliefs," most of which are false. Love is an expression of truth whereas fear is the result of illusion.

By putting our energy and attention and focusing our lives on the intention of spirit (unconditional love) we can overcome fear (ego).

Two people have been living in you all of your life. One is the ego, garrulous, demanding, hysterical, calculating; the other is the hidden spiritual being, whose still voice of wisdom you have only rarely heard or attended to.

Sogyal Rinpoche: Living and dying

Life cannot be kept captive by ego for ever. At some stage evolution dictates that we will discover that our lives cannot be lived fully and to their purpose when we are governed by the ego. We are driven at one stage or another in our lives to transcend the ego and seek the truth.

Spirit speaks the truth and sets us free:

Possessions

In a hectic life dedicated to material gain and status, the voice of spirit becomes faint.

Spirit urges us to recognise that all physical, sensory objects and possessions are temporary and perishable. Fame or integrity – which is more important?

Money or happiness – which is more valuable? Success or failure – which is more destructive? It is the Buddhists' belief that attachment is the source of all suffering in the world.

If we look to others for fulfillment we will never truly be fulfilled. If our happiness depends on money, we will never be happy with ourselves.

We came into this world with nothing and we leave with nothing. We have to accept that happiness cannot be obtained through external objects. "Acquiring possessions" is trying to fill the gap inside of us with objects, and that will never create happiness. We need to find that place within and fill the void with love, peace and contentment for ourselves and others and this will bring new joy into our lives.

When we truly love and value ourselves we will find that we feel less need to supersede ourselves with external possessions. We will see beauty in different places – in spirit, and in nature. We will come to recognise that there is beauty in everybody and everything.

All transformation involves a process of going within and connecting with spirit. Only then can we seek the truth and find the satisfaction and fulfillment we have been seeking. It is in sharing as opposed to gathering that joy is attained. Spirit rejoices with the success of others and feels their joy. When we connect to spirit we come to the realisation that we are all complete, perfect and acceptable just as we are and we do not have to spend our lives trying to prove our worth. We are all divine creations and we do not need material possessions to fulfill the emptiness we feel within. We just need to learn to love ourselves. When we have an inner sense of being complete and whole, knowing that spirit is alive and within all of us, then ego (or fear) will no longer dictate how we feel as it did when we were unknown to spirit.

No quantity of possessions will ever satisfy the ego. We are trying to fill a sense of incompleteness that we feel within ourselves and that can only be done from the inside.

When we practice giving some of our things away, we realise the pleasure we feel that comes with doing that.

> A wise man does not lay up his own treasures. The more
> he gives to others the more he has for his own.
>
> Lao Tzu

Be an example of truth and teach our children that we live in a world full of beauty; we are all unique and beautiful and we do not need to accumulate possessions to fulfill happiness.

> If you realise that you have enough, you are truly rich.
>
> Lao Tzu

Achievements

We need to have faith in ourselves. We are human beings, not human doers. Failure is fiction, every attempt is a success. There is nothing that we are required to be or do here to be eligible for a life filled with love and fulfillment. We are all worthy of love – because we are all made of spirit, and spirit is love. It is incredibly reassuring when we come to the realisation that our life has meaning, purpose and value not by what we possess or achieve, but simply because we are. We will never achieve happiness by gaining more possessions or achieving more goals, because for every desire we fulfill another desire will replace it. This is the nature of life. Spirit thinks of happiness as something that is experienced rather that something that is achieved in many ways every day. Thus we realise the quest for happiness is not external but is all contained within ourselves.

> When you are content to be simply yourself and don't
> compare or compete, everyone will respect you.
>
> Lao Tzu

Be an example of truth and teach our children that they don't have to compete to be the best and win to be acceptable. As long as what we experience is enjoyable and satisfying, and we accept ourselves as who we are, then that is all that matters.

Arrogance

The next time we are in conflict with another, we need to ask ourselves – would I rather be right – or would I rather be happy? We are all so concerned with being right and doing the right thing. We are afraid of being judged each time we make a mistake. Ego automatically reverts back to defensiveness but that just creates more conflict between us. Our strengths lie in our defencelessness.

We can let go of the need to be right and just relax – knowing what we need to know without having to argue with others. Spirit knows that in order to learn, we must make mistakes and it really is alright. We must accept ourselves as what we are – human beings. We show our true spirit when we can accept our mistakes and learn from them. Spirit is not attached to any one point of view, instead can always see things with a different perspective.

> To realise that you do not understand is a virtue; not to realise that you do not understand is a defect.
>
> Lao Tzu

Be an example of truth and teach our children that it is alright to make mistakes and not to punish them or show them rejection in doing so. Show them that mistakes are learning implements that pave the way to success.

Trust

While ego is a host to mistrust – spirit heeds us to trust in the process of life. Trust is a form of approval and approval is one of the strongest motivators there is. Spirit believes that there are no accidents and everything happens for a reason. We need to trust that everything that happens will be of great benefit to us and that life will always give us whatever experience we need for the growth of our soul.

Sometimes it may appear that the experiences we have are unfortunate or hurtful, but if we realise that we will benefit from whatever happens to us, and it will eventually be revealed to us, then we can relax and know that it is a blessing.

So we can let go of the belief that the universe is an unsafe place. We can relax in the knowledge that we are all being guided by a light that is always with us.

When we have the assurance that the world and everything in it is operating from a place of purpose we can let go of our firm grasp on life.

We can let peace and joy replace anxiety and tension.

We automatically trust in the invisible force that is breathing air through our bodies, beating our hearts, birthing our children, changing our seasons and all the other incredible mysteries of life that we seem to take for granted. We need to trust that without recovering the memory of our larger connection, our divine intelligence, we know that the unconditional love of our creator will always be with us here on earth. This knowledge will ultimately lead to a calm, contented peace of mind that knows that the world is under the care of a power much greater than all of us. When we learn to trust ourselves, we trust in the wisdom that created us, so let us trust in that – let go and let God.

> Life is a series of natural and spontaneous changes. Don't resist them; that only creates sorrow. Let reality be reality. Let things flow naturally forward in whatever way they like.
>
> Lao Tzu

> Every child comes into this world in a state of perfection
> They are new arrivals in form only;
> Their true essence is a piece of the infinite consciousness
> that we call by many names
> The most common being "God".
>
> Buckminster Fuller

Be an example of truth and teach our children that everything happens for a reason and everything that happens is always for our benefit – it may not be evident at the time – but it will become apparent at some later stage.

Reputation

When we stop letting other people's opinions dictate who we think we are, an incredibly liberating feeling encloses us – we realise that we are the only ones in control of who we think we are. The only thing that matters is what we think of ourselves. We need to stop comparing ourselves with others and stop creating our beliefs about ourselves by what we think others think about us.

We give our power away when we let other people's opinions control our behaviour.

We need to become self aware, to understand that we are in control of who we want to be by our thoughts and it cannot be governed by an outside force. We need to be authentic and love and accept ourselves unconditionally now, have the courage to allow other people to see the real us, and we will lose the need to seek other people's approval. When we are in spirit we will understand that there is nobody we have to be except exactly who we are being right now.

When we focus on spirit we are reminded that we all came from the same universal intelligence which has no need to concern itself with needing to impress or with the external status symbols of our lives. We are all special in our own way and we are worthy and deserving just because we are here. Love asks nothing in return and is secure enough in itself that it does not fear judgment. Therefore we don't have to do anything or prove anything to anybody else. We were born into love and we all have the opportunity to live a fun, loving, fulfilled and peaceful life.

So we can let go of the limiting beliefs and become aware of who we truly are – a magnificent free spirit who was created in the name of grace and placed on this earth to experience love.

> Embrace simplicity – be content with what you have and
> are, and no one can despoil you.
>
> Tao Te Ching

Be an example of truth and teach our children that it is their God-given right to be who they want to be. They won't worry so much about other people's opinions if they are taught to love and respect themselves first and foremost.

Appearance

Spirit recognises the fact that we are spirits having a human experience rather than humans having a spiritual experience. To think that our physical appearance is our complete being is to deny our innermost being. If we believe that looking a certain way physically is the key to self-love then we have completely disconnected from spirit. Spirit recognises that physical appearances do not make us happy or popular and that we do not have to conform to society's ridiculous expectations of what we should look like in order to be acceptable. Our bodies are not our identity. The body by itself has no purpose. The physical body is the illusion of the ego. The body's only purpose is to house our spirit on this sacred journey. It is an implement that spirit uses to express itself in its physical embodiment. Spirit realises that the body is a mechanism for us to learn from. It is the means by which we experience life. Our ultimate goal is to connect to our original spirit and through our body we can identify whether or not we are on the correct path. We learn through our thoughts and feelings, health and disease and good and bad experiences. Spirit knows that there is so much more to us than our physical attributes and five senses. The way of the spirit is to reflect our inner reality rather than the outer illusion. Spirit's focus is on developing our inner beauty so that it can be reflected in everything we do and what we are to become; therefore spirit knows that true beauty comes from the inside. Spirit recognises that we are not here as a separate body among bodies, rather a spirit among spirits.

Our lives are ultimately a collection of experiences and we are a memory of our reaction to those experiences. The ego believes in body identification. It believes that all we are is this physical body. This keeps us feeling small and limited. We see ourselves as encapsulated in one very separate identity, separated from everything and everybody else. The greatest discovery is that we are more than our mind and our body. We are pure spirit.

The new testament tells us that we are IN this world but not OF this world. Therefore if we can discard our identification with our bodies we can detach ourselves from ego.

> Your body is nothing more than the garage where you temporarily park your soul.
>
> Wayne Dyer

Be an example of truth and teach our children that true beauty is invisible and unaware of its own beauty. Who they are is what is on the inside – who we are is our own beautiful spirit– as opposed to our physical bodies.

Limitations

We came from divine source – timeless, joyful, eternal and free from all limitations. Real power is the power to create, the power to transform, the power to heal, the power to love, and the power to be free. Real power comes from our connection to our deepest self; to our spirit.

Our spiritual beings are boundless. The spiritual self has no restrictions. It is the ego that puts limitations on ourselves. We are pure potentiality. When we know and understand that we are completely free, without limitations we recognise our lives as a source of infinite possibilities. We can then realise that every intention, every desire and every dream that we ever had can be fulfilled.

When we listen to spirit we know that we are not limited by the five physical senses. Limitations are what we experience when we identify ourselves as only a physical body in material existence. Spirit represents that which we cannot validate with our five senses. The ego draws our mind outward to the material and physical aspects of our lives while spirit draws our minds inwards. We are in fact multi-sensory. We know that there is so much more to us than the physical body. We know that we are all connected to the divine light and we all operate from the one mind. Therefore we are always communicating with spirit and listening to our spiritual intuition which when we are aware, is guiding us through life, leading us to our inquiries – what we need to experience and what we need to acknowledge.

We know that we are in charge of our lives and have the ability to change the way we think, therefore construct our lives in any way, shape or form. The power is in our own hands and so we are not limited – we are indeed more powerful than we have ever given ourselves credit for. When we know that we are in the presence of divine intelligence we know that everything that happens in this lifetime happens for a specific reason and that everything that happens to us is always for our greatest benefit.

When we know that we are being watched over and guided, we can feel safe and trust in the knowledge that whatever happens to us will always be to our full advantage and that we are never alone in this lifetime. The universe is complete and perfect it is entirety.

> Whether you think you will succeed or not, you are right.
> Henry Ford

Be an example of truth and teach our children that they are not limited by anything. They have the power to change their thoughts, therefore change their lives. They can do whatever they set their minds to do – anywhere, anyhow, anyplace and anytime.

Time

The point of power can only be in the present moment. The present moment is all we have. Guilt over the past is a complete waste of energy – it will never change the outcome and will only make us feel inferior. The past has no power over the present moment. The ego is completely conditioned by the past.

Worry over the future is as much a waste of energy. There is nothing that we can accomplish by worrying about the future. Only ego speculates about tomorrow.

What we need to do is concentrate and enjoy being in the present moment. This is where we spend the least amount of time and the only place where ego doesn't exist! The only place the ego CAN exist is in the past or the future.

The only way to let go of pain is to live in the 'now' so we need to make the 'now' the primary focus of our life. When we give our full attention to what is happening in the present moment we discover that all there is, is contained within this very moment. This is a miraculous journey that we are on and it is happening to us NOW. When we understand this we will feel pure satisfaction without the effects of time. The past is over and the future hasn't happened yet. When we stop worrying about the future, and feeling guilty about the past, we can relax and enjoy the peace of the present moment now. When we are physically in one place, but mentally in another, we are essentially missing out on our own lives.

Being present in the moment of now ensures that the ego is not present. Being in the present moment is the ONLY place where miracles (a shift in perception from fear to spirit) happen.

> The past has no power to stop you from being present now.
> Only your grievance about the past can do that. What is
> grievance? The baggage of old thought and emotion.
>
> Lao Tzu

In order to be free we have to let go of our past personal histories. By being tied to our personal history we prohibit ourselves the presence of NOW. By allowing our personal histories to define us as individuals we inhibit our personal growth process. When we can let go of our personal histories we find that we have nothing to live up to. The standards that we have set for ourselves no longer restrict us. We become free in ourselves when we no longer rely on the way that things have always been to define how our lives will be today. We have the ability to erase our past and all the limitations that have become our beliefs. We can let go of all those beliefs that convince us of our inadequacies and inferiority complexes. When we discover that we don't need our personal histories any longer and we can let them go, we recognise that all the people, circumstances and events that have happened are all part of the ever unfolding, changing and growing tale of our lives and with every new day comes the opportunity to open ourselves up to a clear new perspective – a clean slate – and create anew. We realise that we are free to have an open mind about the endless possibilities available to us in the present moment of NOW. We make up our own mind, therefore we create our own reality.

> To be born again is to let the past go, and look without condemnation upon the present. You are asked to let the future go, and place it in God's hands. And you will see by your experiences that you have laid the past and the present in His hands as well, because the past will punish you no more, and the future dread will now be meaningless.
>
> A Course in Miracles

When we are at peace with spirit we can trust that all is well. Everything is happening for a reason and whenever we disagree with it we experience anxiety and frustration. Any thought that causes stress to ourselves is a disagreement with spirit. The ego thinks that things should be different than what they are. It will always hurt when we argue with "What is". This is the ego trying to change the past. The past cannot be changed and it is only when we listen to spirit's guiding voice telling us where to go from here that we can attain any peace. When we can just allow it to happen we will stop judging the past as "good" or "bad". The past is a teacher – whatever has happened, it is all linked in some way to our divine plan. We needed that experience to help us overcome a certain challenge, to help us learn and grow as individuals on our spiritual path. We need to understand that the people that are in our lives are here to teach us and each other to develop as divine beings. It a part of the chapter of the story of our lives and is a necessary part of who we are today. The past is there as an opportunity, presenting us with a life lesson, but the ego is dedicated to changing the past. As long as we are questioning the past, we are living in the past. Comparing what happened with what we think should have happened is to be at war with spirit. When we believe that the past should have been different we create anger and tension. And we keep attracting anger and tension into our lives because what we resist persists. Our stressful reality remains. But for the ego, which is attached to right and wrong, comparison will always precede. The more we react in ego or negative energy to the opportunities presented to us in life, the more similar opportunities will be presented to us as catalysts for our learning experiences.

Living in spirit will free us from the pain of discrepancies with the past and what the ego thinks should have happened as opposed to accepting with grace that everything happens for a reason. Ego is trying to manipulate reality and that will always create unhappiness.

When we experience adversity and can react in an attitude of acceptance we will experience a sudden, clear resonance that everything is happening for a reason and that is crucial to the unfolding of our lesson in the story of our life. Once we stop the ego disagreeing with the situation, whatever it may be, we have the ability to see the situation for what it really is and the anxiety fades away. We begin to see with clarity reality for what it really is – profound and immense. We realise what the experience is there to teach us and we come to the conclusion that the stressful situation that we perceived it to be is in fact the greatest gift that we could ever receive. We begin to understand the matrix behind the reality. We finally understand the illusion that the ego believes when it tells us "it shouldn't have happened that way".

We can do nothing about the past; it has been and gone. No amount of sadness, regret or prayer can change what has already happened in the past, nor will punishing ourselves for year upon year bring about any change, and any discrepancies about that will only bring about internal conflict. When we can accept with gratitude the things that have happened and see the power and truth in our own unfolding life story can we fully realise the intelligence of the universal energy life force that is creating our lives day after day.

We can do nothing about the future. It is not here yet. But today is ours to use in whatever way we choose. Today is the beginning through which the future will emerge.

Ego bases its perception of reality on what has happened in the past and then carries those perceptions into the present and thus creates a future – much like the present. This is the cycle that needs to be broken. We need to detach ourselves from past-future preoccupations and choose to live in the now. Spirit returns our mind to total faith and trust in the present moment. All there ever was and all there will ever be is in the now. The present moment is all that exists.

When we dwell on the past it draws our attention away from what is happening in the present moment. It ensures that each of our subsequent life experiences will be tainted by the trauma of whatever was once said or done, which will in turn trigger negative feelings, which will endorse negative behaviour and choices, which will create more negative manifestations. What we think about becomes real. What we cause, we effect and the bitter will grow more bitter. Dwelling on what once hurt us in the past will bring about new losses, more disappointments and new reasons to feel hurt and pain.

Awareness of the ego is concealed within the point of power that is in the present moment. When we master this major concept, peace begins to enter our lives, and peace is ultimately the end of ego.

> Your mission is very simple. You are asked to live as so to demonstrate that you are not an ego. If you are not feeling a deep, rich sense of yourself and your purpose in now-here, it is probably because you believe you are your ego.
>
> A Course in Miracles

Be an example of truth and teach our children not to feel guilty about what happened in the past and not to feel worry about the future. Notice, experience, in our reality the utter perfection of the present moment. The present moment is all we have control of so we need to live in the now.

> If you are depressed you are living in the past
> If you are anxious you are living in the future
> If you are at peace you are living in the present.
>
> Lao Tzu

Unity

We are all here to awaken from the illusion that we are all separate. Other than our personalities and egos encapsulated by our physical bodies, we are all created from the same universal source. We are all related. We are all in harmony, loved and never alone.

Think about spirit being the deep and vast ocean and us as being a river that connects to it. We are not as big, or as powerful, but we all come from the same source. We are all born from the one thing, and will return to the one thing. Each river is different, but they all eventually lead to the ocean. No matter what we are doing, whether it bring us happiness or misery, we are all on a path back to spirit. We are all on a journey to enlightenment.

We are not separate from spirit. Everything is interconnected – all energy and all consciousness. There are no separate objects or separate beings. Separation is an illusion. We are as integral to, and inseparable from, the universe as are the stars, the mountains and oceans and everything else that exists. There is unity in all creation.

When we can look at the world and see it as pure energy, we realise that we are not just solid beings. We are vibratory beings. There is no distinction between mind and matter; it is pure energy. Whether it is visible energy such as our body, or an invisible energy such as a thought or radio wave – we are all made of the same thing. There is no separation.

Deep down we always yearn for our lost sense of oneness, of wholeness, of spirit. We have somehow lost the light, and lost touch with love, wonderment, joy and delight.

We are created as a likeness to spirit and we only have to look inside to communicate with spirit. We need to listen to our feelings, thoughts and experiences – this is our most dependable guide.

We are always in contact with spirit as spirit is inside all of us. In the pure consciousness state – we are all universal energy. Each of us is connected to this universal energy – we just need to be willing to acknowledge and listen. The only thing keeping us from an awareness of this is the ego. You will know the difference between ego and spirit – spirit's voice will be truthful – you will feel and know the truth – it will be clear and precise and it will be in the name of love, joy, fulfillment and it will resonate with you. Your instinct (spirit) will tell you that it is right.

Spirit is consciousness. Spirit is the source of creation itself. It is not independent of us; it is the totality of everything. So when we call ourselves spirit we are talking about the expression of the spirit self that resides within each and every one of us. Spirit is an energy. Spirit is a VERB. Spirit is not a noun, person or thing. When we believe that spirit is a person place or thing, we separate ourselves from it and we immediately become a limited being. This is what separates the religious or the believers from the spiritual or the knowing.

Blasphemy is the theory that spirit is a separate entity. The ego's belief that we are somehow separate from spirit is the cause of every destructive or negative consequence in the universe. The cure is the knowledge that nothing can separate us from spirit.

Separation is the great illusion. Albert Einstein called it "the great optical illusion of consciousness". There is no separation between us and spirit. Separation is the great disease of mankind. Because we believe that we are separate from each other, from our source and from ourselves, we experience lack, struggle, conflict, pain and disease. When we divide the whole and call it "yours" and "mine" we feel estranged, separate and disassociated from everybody and everything. The feeling of separation evokes suspicion, fear, defensiveness, competitiveness, envy and attack. We treat life as a competition – we compete to see who has the most and because we do not extend love to anything that does not belong to us we suffer even more. The ego sees us as separate and separation from spirit causes pain and unhappiness. Because we see life as being separate from other people we take on an us versus them, or us versus God attitude.

> A sense of separation from God is the only lack you really need to correct.
>
> A Course in Miracles

When we see ourselves as connected to everybody else, we cease our judgment and compassion becomes an automatic reaction. We see the world as one entity and rather than acting as competitors or traitors we react in love rather than defence. Our identification moves away from our differences and we begin to see our commonalities. Appearance no longer becomes important as our priorities begin to change and fear and hatred is replaced by spirit – a desire to resolve what divides us as human beings.

We will stop labeling ourselves and categorising ourselves as "us" versus "them".

There is no existence of a God as depicted by nearly every religion.

Spirit (God) is the sum of all that is; it is every voice, every heartbeat, every man woman and child, every animal and every rock. What is God not? Nothing. The ego will not allow us to see beyond the five senses but spirit knows the truth because it runs transient with us; it resonates with us. There is a universal intelligence behind our lives that we cannot see or touch that opens the roses, grows our fingernails and sets the sun in the evenings. Spirit is the creator of everything and all of that intelligence is born into each creation of that intelligence thus the universal mind is integrated within each and every one of us. We all have within us the divine universal intelligence. The truth is who we are is a part of everything in the universe – the infinite intelligence. We are not separate. We just need to awaken to the power and perfection that is within us all. When we become aware of this, we can change our lives. When we recognise our own infinity we become free. We can revel in the glory of being one with the divine. We will know that we are all eternal souls taking on human form for a brief time; death is just a passageway into another existence where we will return to our spirit selves. We can heal by returning to the brilliant love of light that is always within us and know that we are always safe.

Be an example of truth and teach our children about the miraculous art of creation, that spirit resides in us all and that as humanity we are never alone.

Existence is beyond the power of words to define. Whether a man dispassionately sees to the core of life or passionately sees the surface, the core and the surface are essentially the same, words making them seem different, only to express appearance. If name be needed, wonder names them both; from wonder into wonder existence opens.

Lao Tzu

Judgment

The antidote to judgment is acceptance. When we can accept the situation or experience as reality and let it go, we will be working with spirit.

All of us are here living our miraculously unique journeys, so to compare and judge where we have been, what we are doing and what we have in relation to each other is a complete and utter waste of our time and energy.

When we have the sincerity to restore good wishes on the other person instead of judgment we will not only free them, but free ourselves. Everybody is unique, and we all bring our own uniqueness to share with the world which makes every one of us special. Diversity and contrast is what gives everybody their own perceptions and their ability to see the world from a different point of view. Spirit does not judge and nor should we.

Spirit informs us that we all originate from the same divine source which is pure unconditional love. There is no bad or evil, therefore there is nothing to judge.

We need to remove the word "should" from our vocabularies. The word "should" implies that we are or were wrong. We need to replace it with the word "could". This gives us choice and choice is freedom.

When we judge others we deny the presence of spirit in them.

When we really think about it, the difference between a rose and its thorn is just a judgment. If we can accept some new concepts into our lives, and see that as an opportunity to expand our reality and grow as spirit, then judgment becomes irrelevant.

Be an example of truth and teach our children that we are all special and each of us brings our unique gifts to the world and instead of being judgmental toward our differences, be accepting and gracious of the lessons we may learn.

Forgiveness

Forgiveness allows spirit to take back its control. Our peace of mind is more important that any negative act inflicted on us. Our emotional self is at the core of who we are and we carry that around with us every minute of every day. If our emotional self is full of pain, anger, hurt and resentment, that ultimately is who we will become and how our life will become. The inevitable resentment and rancour associated with not letting go or working through resentments will eventually incorporate into our own thoughts and emotions on a much larger scale. These feelings will begin to take over and thus become a part of who we are. Our life experiences, more so the interpretation that we extract from those life experiences become our manual that ultimately guides us through our life.

When we choose to hold onto our resentments we are choosing to stay in continuous pain. We are living our lives according to somebody else's mistake. We are instigating our own pain and grief by not letting go. It undermines our health and our joy in living. It certainly does not benefit us or the other person to lock ourselves into a cycle of blame and resentment. We can often therefore take over where they left off and continue to berate ourselves until long after the other person has forgotten. We stew in our own poison and continue to contaminate those around us.

> Sometimes letting things go is an act of far greater power
> than defending or hanging on.
>
> Eckhart Tolle

To cast blame means not to understand that we create our own reality and this can rob us of our power to live deliberately for today. It prevents us from accepting responsibility for creating the rest of our lives. When there is blame, there is a belief that bad things can happen to us for no apparent reason.

Forgiveness is empowering ourselves to act in our own best interests. Rather than waiting for another person to change so that we can feel better about ourselves, we can take control. Forgiveness is a self deserving act. When we stop carrying around the huge rage of resentment, anger and hatred, we will feel like a burden has been lifted from our shoulders. It is a choice to stop living in the past and let go of all attachment to hurt, pain, fear and resentment. It allows us a sense of freedom when we are able to move beyond our innermost blocks.

Forgiveness is not about condoning the other person's painful behaviour, or "letting them off the hook". We may choose to never see that person again. We do not forgive for the sake of the other person, we forgive as a gift to ourselves. When we come to the decision to simply let it go, to stop carrying it around with us and letting it affect our everyday life, we will find peace within. We simply come to the point where we stop letting the past dictate our future. It is about hitting the reset button.

When we are ready to forgive, we are ready to reject the possibility that the rest of our lives will be determined by the unjust and hurtful acts of another person. Forgiveness of ourselves and of others allows us to embrace our own and others' imperfections so that we are able to release the pain. The bitterness and rancour that we are carrying around inside is doing us more harm than them. We need to question whether holding onto a grudge or waiting for our moment of revenge is worth the internal anxiety. When we forgive we let go of all the resentment, anger and hurt. We realise that we have been carrying around this unnecessary burden for a long time and it has had many negative impacts on our lives. To forgive is to set a prisoner free and then discover that the prisoner was us all along.

Forgiveness is learning to make peace with what we have been given as opposed to being angry and resentful at what we haven't been given. The cost of being angry and resentful is always to the victim. In holding anyone to blame we limit our own growth. Our own hurt and pain is destroying ourselves.

Of all the years that we wait for them to make it up to us and of all of the energy that we extend trying to make them change, or to seek revenge, all we succeed in achieving is to keep the old wounds from healing and give pain from the past permission to dominate our lives and damage our lives. And they still may not have changed. Nothing we can ever do will make them change. They may never change. The person who broke us cannot be the person to fix us. Inner peace is found by changing ourselves, not the person who hurt us. And we change ourselves for peace of mind, understanding, compassion and from the pain of the past. We do not need to live at the other end of somebody's mistake – when we do, it just becomes our mistake too. We do not need to take up residence in another person's problem. We need to restore ourselves – to get whole and acquire a sense of joy and freedom. When we hold resentment toward another, we are bound to that person or condition by an emotional link that is stronger than steel. Forgiveness is the only way to dissolve that link and be free. When we cannot forgive and move on, the damage will be evident in our own lives. We doom ourselves to repeat the same painful experiences that debilitate our happiness.

A Course in Miracles says that all disease comes from a state of unforgiving.

Storing negative emotions cause disease. Emotions are the end product of past experiences. They become twisted and lodged in the anatomy of our bodies and make us sick. Illnesses are connected to mind and body. Anger shows up in the liver, grief in the lungs and resentment eats away at the body and can cause cancer.

We need to recognise that the negative emotions that we have stored are memories from our past experiences.

We need to consider whether these negative emotions are still significant in our lives now and if we will let those emotions dictate how we live our lives today.

To spend a lifetime reliving the same feelings of blame, anger and resentment is only inflicting unnecessary pain onto ourselves.

To forgive is to let go of all negativity and free ourselves from all the hurt of the past. We need to realise that the past is over and we cannot change the past but we can change our thinking about the past. How ridiculous is it to punish ourselves in the present moment because somebody hurt us in the past. We need to let go and return to the present moment.

Letting go is a release of the past; a decision to not have it burden our present or future any longer. We could look at it as a funeral of the experience. We release the power that it holds in our everyday lives. We move it from the foreground to the background. We are ready to move on. We can take stock of our lives and let go of the emotional burdens. We can then feel free to make choices that have less to do with the past and more to do with the present. Forgiveness is letting go of the belief that the past could have been different. It is acceptance of what is. We cannot change the past and any amount of speculation on the subject will just inflict more suffering. When we forgive we will have the ability to think more clearly as we have removed our emotional baggage. Forgiveness is necessary for us to become the person that we were intended to be. It is the only way to true wholeness and happiness. It is the only way to freedom. An unforgiven injury binds us to a time and a place that somebody else has created and chosen. It holds us trapped in a past moment in our past feelings. Forgiveness is part of the process of letting go and moving on. Growth is essential in this lifetime and forgiveness and restoring inner peace paves the way for growth to occur.

The person who is the hardest to forgive is the one who can teach us the greatest lessons. When we love ourselves enough to rise above the old situation, then understanding and forgiveness will be easy. Forgiveness is liberation.

When we realise that getting angry about something is not going to change the outcome, or serve us in any way, only inflict negativity onto ourselves and others, we can skip the process and move straight to spirit.

Even more important than learning how to forgive other people is learning how to forgive ourselves. There is a big difference between holding ourselves accountable for our actions in a mature way – knowing that the mistakes that we have made pave the way for lessons learned in life, as opposed to tearing ourselves up inside. Owning up to our mistakes and taking responsibility for them is far beyond condemning ourselves and reprimanding ourselves. Be compassionate about any mistakes or regrets we have. Understand that those mistakes were made for a reason and learn the lesson instead of feeling guilt and shame. The lessons are all a part of the journey of our lives and we need to accept our flaws as well as our strengths.

Forgive those moments of the past for all we think we "should" or "shouldn't" have done. Constantly reminding ourselves about the completely shameful incident ten years ago is giving in to guilt. Guilt is a useless emotion. Let it go. Let go of the ego's shameful taunts. Give ourselves permission to begin again. The universe provides us with a clean slate on which to write at any given moment.

As we begin to look at ourselves and our lives in a more compassionate way, it becomes easier for us to forgive our mistakes and with forgiveness we are able to heal and with that healing comes empowerment.

Forgiveness gives us inner peace, releasing the toxic feelings inside. It is not worth sacrificing our inner tranquility in order to maintain negative feelings. In letting go, we forgive ourselves and realise that we all deserve inner peace.

Forgiveness feels like a huge weight has been lifted from our shoulders. Suddenly we feel completely free – free from all that negativity and chaos. We realise that by listening to the ego and refusing to forgive, the only one that we were truly punishing and imprisoning was ourselves.

Forgiveness is one of the most powerful forces in the universe. It will release old pain and by releasing negative energy it will create room for more positive energy in our lives. Once forgiveness had been made to those in the past, our future will be changed and transformed. The act of forgiveness allows us to let go of our wounds and wipes our past slate clean. Without forgiveness our lives are identified by our wounds and spiritual growth becomes impossible. Forgiveness frees us to be able to react and respond in the present moment, rather than reacting from past wounds. It clears our vision so that we are able to see from a different perspective the truth of the situation rather than from the perspective of our past pain.

> Forgiveness is the fragrance that the violet sheds on the heel that has crushed it.
>
> Mark Twain

Be an example of truth and teach our children that forgiveness is really the gift of freedom that only we can give to ourselves.

Gratitude

Gratitude is another form of love. When we are grateful for our life we are using love as an expression to thank spirit for the life that it has given to us.

The fastest and most efficient way of restoring harmony and balance in our lives is by incorporating gratitude and appreciation into our lives.

Love is the power that heals our lives, and love is the power that will ultimately heal the world. Gratitude is another form of love, a natural expression of a loving heart. Therefore whenever we express gratitude, we align ourselves with the power that heals us. Feeling gratitude spreads healing energy and gives the world a more positive energy. When we express gratitude we raise the vibrations around us to a higher frequency. We create positive energy that emanates outward and returns positive energy back to us. Every time we express appreciation, we help heal the world.

Gratitude expands our vision and gives us the power to change challenges into possibilities, problems into solutions and negatives into positives.

Gratitude is an access to awareness, and awareness is the path to love. It is what gives life its meaning. It enables us to feel the full potential of life. Gratitude is a powerful attitude that will move us from a feeling of limitation and fear to one of expansion and love. When we view life as a gift and consequently acquire an "attitude of gratitude" we will see our lives change in many positive areas. Gratitude will elevate, inspire and transform our lives to a much greater meaning.

The ego (fear) does not exist where there is gratitude. The ego thrives on dissatisfaction and ungratefulness, while the spirit lives in gratitude. While we are in the presence of genuine gratitude, it is impossible to feel fear, worry, anger or depression, therefore we cannot be grateful and unhappy at the same time.

When we are in the state of gratitude, we reverse the pattern of looking outwardly for any kind of satisfaction to generating happiness from the inside – where spirit resides. Our ability to enjoy life comes from how we choose to perceive life. Nothing outside of ourselves has the power to create happiness or fulfillment. We have the power within us to create the sort of world in which we want to live. Having this knowledge, we realise that a life filled with contentment is readily available to us all, no matter what the external circumstances. And when we cultivate a life filled with compassion and gratitude, we will never feel alone or dissatisfied.

> As we express our gratitude, we must never forget that the highest appreciation is not to utter words, but to live by them.
>
> John F Kennedy

Gratitude is the antidote to criticism. When we feel gratitude we receive a sudden awareness of a deep compassion and appreciation for the world and everything in it. We are the recipients of the honorary gift of life, and when we change our perspective to realising that there are so many more positive things about our life as opposed to all the negative things, we become truly grateful. We develop a greater appreciation for all that we have and all that we are, and we feel the true value of the simple things in life. Happiness comes by embracing the journey of life and being grateful for every thought, feeling, experience or event we are experiencing in the present moment. We realise that there is a fundamental quality in just being alive and we can stop and appreciate all the love, beauty and blessings in our life – simply breathing in the cold winter air and feeling our aliveness, the spring blossoms, the sun on our back or a pot of soup on the stove in winter time. No matter what our situation is, there are always moments of beauty and joy where we have the opportunity to live our lives with inner joy and gratitude.

When we truly feel gratitude, we are able to fully experience and embrace the spontaneity of a moment that is not sought after or even anticipated.

When we simplify our lives to that degree, we can become profoundly grateful for the little things in life and we can truly appreciate all that this world is. We can release the worry and anxiety and watch the criticisms and dissatisfaction disappear.

As we awaken to our divine nature we will begin to appreciate beauty in everything that we see, touch and experience.

Everything that happens in our lifetime happens for a reason, and everything that happens to us is for our greatest benefit; therefore every occurrence is a blessing.

When we know this to be true, all of the fear, frustration and anger simply disappears. Gratitude becomes an automatic response to anything that happens to us and gratitude is followed by peace, joy and happiness.

> There is no disaster greater than not being content.
>
> Lao Tzu

Gratitude is not the result of things that happen to us – it is an attitude that we ourselves cultivate. The more that we are grateful for, the more that we will attract things to be grateful for. We can look at any experience in two ways: With the perception of deficiency; or with the perception of abundance. Ego sees limitations while spirit sees possibilities. Each attitude will be justified by the belief system that we hold to be true. The life that we perceive from our consciousness will be the life that we will ultimately lead. If we change our allegiance from ego (fear) to love (spirit), we can be assured that spirit will nurture us through whatever we choose to experience in this lifetime.

> Love cannot be far behind a grateful heart and a thankful mind. These are the true conditions of your homecoming.
>
> A Course in Miracles

The wisdom of gratitude contains the solutions to most of our damaging experiences and situations. It is the primary emotion that can elevate us through all hardships and challenges. Feeling grateful is the defining characteristic of grace within our human experience because it holds within it the principles of justice and faith.

Experiencing gratitude is the most effective way of staying connected with spirit. When we are connected to spirit we hear the thoughts of the universe. It is one of the secrets of living a completely fulfilled life. We feel connected to everything in creation and we feel a huge sense of clarity and vision. Gratitude is a fullness of heart that moves us from a deep dissatisfaction to a deep appreciation of all things, most of all ourselves.

When we finally understand that our physical bodies and this lifetime were both honorary gifts from spirit – a gift to be eternally thankful for – then can we truly embrace the gift of gratitude.

When we experience an ongoing grateful attitude we find that compassion also becomes an automatic response to people, circumstances and events. Compassion is the joy of giving and sharing. It is the small things that we do and share with other people. Sharing a smile or a small act of kindness on our behalf can do more for the soul than many monetary offerings. We find that instead of continuously repeating ego's mantra of "how much can I acquire" we find solace in spirit's voice that asks from a core of unconditional love, "how may I serve others?"

> The fruit of love is service, which is compassion in action. Religion has nothing to do with compassion, it is our love for God that is the main thing because we have all been created for the soul purpose to love and be loved.
> Mother Teresa: For the love of God

When gratitude and compassion become a natural way of life we find that all aspects – physical, spiritual and material begin to co-exist simultaneously. Borders of separation within us dissolve into understanding and awareness of our unity with each other and the universe. Having a deep knowing that everything happens for a reason and everything that happens to us is for our utmost benefit, we find that the stumbling blocks that used to lead to our lessons, have transformed into stepping stones, through which cascades a gentle stream of water.

> I have just three things to teach: Simplicity, patience and compassion. These three are your greatest treasures.
> Lao Tzu

Gratitude is our acknowledgment to spirit that we are aware of its presence. We are aware of the divine intelligence presence that is guiding us, holding us and protecting us. The practice of gratitude is an offering that creates a field of resonance that unifies and empowers our vision of personal and global transformation.

Being in a state of gratitude allows us to see things in perspective. Gratitude has the power to transform any situation from negative to positive and is the most powerful way to cause changes in our lives as compassion and understanding replace fear and sorrow.

Each day when we open the curtains of our life we can know that our creator has given us the gift of another day, another chance to begin anew, learn something new, laugh, delight, rejoice and love in this wonderful realm of humanity. When we learn to come from a place of gratitude frustration gives way to appreciation and joy and peace begin to prevail.

Be an example and teach our children to notice acts of kindness, beauty, blessings and people, and to appreciate and be grateful for them. To never take people, circumstances or situations for granted, to know that everything happens for a reason, each experience has a message and every person is in our lives to teach us something, and to always seek out the positive.

> Be content with what you have; rejoice in the way things are. When you realise there is nothing lacking, the world belongs to you.
>
> Lao Tzu

Chapter three
THE POWER OF THE MIND

If you correct your mind – the rest of your life will fall into place.

Lao Tzu

It is through the mind that everything comes into being. We have this powerful creative energy that creates the thoughts that we think and the words that we speak. Our mind determines the success and happiness or the hurt and suffering of our lives. Our thoughts ultimately create our own experiences. Our experiences create our lives. The world is a projection of our own thinking. Freedom comes when we acknowledge that we are the creators of our own lives. This is one of the most significant and inspiring realisations known to man. It reflects man's divine nature. This is the fundamental prerogative with which we have the power to control our own lives.

Peace, love and joy are fundamentally our core essence. It is what we came from and is therefore what we know to be the truth in our innermost being. Only by believing an untrue thought is it possible to move from peace into emotions like anger or sadness. Without the ego drawing into these negative beliefs the mind would stay in spirit.

Any negative emotion is a sign that we are being drawn into a thought that we know not to be true. It indicates that spirit is being overtaken by ego. Loss of spirit means loss of the awareness of love and the replacement of fear. When the mind is without ego there will be no sadness or anger. We will be completely aligned with peace and the truth of what is. Therefore we cannot suffer unless we believe an untrue belief or thought. Our suffering is caused by believing a prior thought. When we change this thought, our lives will change.

> The greatest discovery of all time is that a person can change his future by merely changing his attitude.
>
> Oprah Winfrey

What is it that we call bad luck? Simply put, bad luck is when our reality isn't equivalent to what we think our reality should be. When our plan doesn't match up to what is actually happening in reality, the negative emotions occur. When we argue that it shouldn't be this way or that it shouldn't be this hard it leads to feeling of anger and disillusionment. Our identity is being defeated. Only when we realise that reality is going to happen with or without our own personal plan can we conform to any sort of acceptance. Accepting things as they are opens us to possibilities we otherwise would not have if we judge people and events as good or bad luck. We can succumb to reality and accept that life's destination is reality and that everything happens for a reason. How can we know that this situation or experience is happening right now for our greatest good? Because that is the experience that we are having right now. When we realise this, we can step back and just accept the joy and beauty around us knowing that life is a journey of growth, not a destination of control.

Being in spirit means understanding and knowing ourselves beyond our plan and being aware of what remains in full appreciation and gratitude. It is the realisation that everything that we are is aligned and part of an integral plan, designed by the universal divine intelligence. Our suffering will end when we let go and let God.

Our whole lives are based on a belief system. Our lives are therefore conducted through our core beliefs – what we believe to be true based on the circumstances and experiences of our lives. The thoughts we believe ultimately direct our lives, therefore we will act in accordance with those beliefs – whatever they may be. When we know this we realise that suffering is optional. We suffer because we believe our thoughts. We suffer because we argue with and distort our view of reality. We argue with what is and what has been. We live in denial. Freedom comes when we question those core beliefs and establish whether they are still current or out of date. We may be holding on to beliefs that we had as a child. When we lose attachments of those concepts and start living independently of these beliefs we will come to a new understanding of ourselves and our world and spirit will begin to return to our lives. We will find the truth and we will experience freedom and happiness.

> Ninety five percent of the beliefs we have stored in our minds are nothing but lies, and we suffer because we believe all these lies.
>
> Don Miguel Ruiz

Nothing happens by chance. Our thoughts and beliefs create our reality. Our thoughts are energy and that energy attracts people, events and opportunities that resonate with that energy. Whatever we believe, desire, fear or expect, we will attract that toward ourselves. There is no luck, fate, chance or coincidence. There are no accidents. There is however synchronicity and intuition.

Day by day, moment by moment we create our own stories. Reality is a frozen thought. The universe is merely a feedback system. It reflects back our own beliefs and attitudes, fears, thoughts, feelings and expectation. The outer world mirrors our inner world. Each of us will attract people or experiences into our lives whose story is in line with ours. Everything is interconnected. Our beliefs create our experiences. To change our experiences we need to change our thoughts.

Forces beyond our control can take away everything that we possess except one thing – our freedom to choose how we will respond to the situation. We cannot control what happens to us, but we can always control how we will respond. We all act in accordance to our beliefs and perceptions about the events, situations and people that occur in our lives.

How we perceive ourselves and the world around us is the result of many years creating our personal perceptions through preconceived notions. Everything that we see, hear and feel is through the filter of our own perception. We only see the part of the concept that our perceptual filter allows us to see and we accept these perceptions as realities. This is how our minds work. Thus we live our lives according to our own self imposed perceptions; therefore nothing has any meaning except the meaning that we give to it.

We as human beings can alter our lives by altering the perceptions of our mind. When we change our way of looking at the world, our thinking and acting changes. The way we feel on the interior will determine how we will behave on the exterior. When we realise that we can change our perceptions, adjust our beliefs and our way of looking at the world, we will develop a new mindset.

Our perspective is a combination of our thoughts, our emotions and our opinions and that determines our perspective of the events and circumstances that are happening in the world around us. Our perception is the determining factor that will ultimately create our lives. We will always be what we perceive ourselves to be until we begin to question our beliefs. Our lives will be lived by the results of all the thoughts, beliefs and experiences that we have had that have created our perception of the world.

Our perception is responsible for how we live our lives and how we respond to the situations and experiences that happen in our lives; and how we respond to the experiences in our lives is ultimately what makes our lives what they are. Therefore our perception is more important than the facts. There are certain facts that cannot be changed, but our perception can always overcome these facts. What we see is only accurate and complete for ourselves. It is our own interpretation.

The opposite of what we know is also true. Every other person's perspective on reality is true for them. It is as valid for them as ours is to us, so no matter how certain we are that what we are doing is "the right or correct way" we must accept the possibility that even somebody doing the exact opposite might be doing "the right or correct thing" as well.

Our interpretation is based on our "internal reality;" our thoughts. Thoughts create the invisible energy around us. The cause of our world are our thoughts. All our experiences are outer expressions of our inner dialogue. We do not see things as they are, we see things as we are.

To maintain a positive perspective we must realise that while we may not be able to control the things that happen around us, or the things that happen to us, we can control the things that happen inside us. Perception is the key and it is always our choice.

Life is not so much about what happens to us, but the way in which we respond to what happens to us.

> How people treat you is their karma
> How you react is yours.
>
> Wayne Dyer

We all have personal responsibility for our reality and the fact that what we think will determine our actions, which will determine our experiences. The real us is not what we see on the exterior, but what we are on the interior. The interior being is the core being of ourselves. The core of the apple is where we find the seeds that grow into the future of that apple; therefore it is the most important part. The same applies to us. The heart or core is where our most intense thoughts, feelings and beliefs are to be found. When we learn how to tap into our true inner selves, we can begin to reveal our true thoughts, dreams, feelings and beliefs. These are the things that we ultimately live our lives by. These are the things that guide, direct, determine and create how we live our lives. This is where and how we determine what we will or will not do in a certain situation, what we will or will not attempt to achieve, and our core beliefs about ourselves and the world. The core is the heart of our centre – our real selves.

We create our lives by what we believe to be true. Our belief system is based on our past experiences, therefore our beliefs are constantly relived in the present moment with an anticipation that the future will hold more of the same.

We create our thoughts through imagination, our thoughts create our ideas, ideas create intentions and intentions create the guidance necessary to cause us to take action.

Imagination – thought – idea – intention – action – reality.

Our thoughts are based on our perceptions – what we choose to believe about ourselves and the world.

Our perceptions come from our thoughts, beliefs and experiences of our lives. Those perceptions can be completely inappropriate but we have allowed those perceptions to enter our mind and give them the power to influence us. When we stop giving these thoughts power, they will cease to happen. Perceptions are manufactured internally and always open to revision. That which we give attention to grows. (As you think so shall you be.) Our input always determines our output so when we change our way of thinking, we can change our lives. When we rid ourselves of the negative beliefs, doubts, fears and perceptions, we can change the outcome of our lives.

If we think positive thoughts, we will produce positive outcomes. If we think negative thoughts we will produce negative outcomes. If we believe that we are destined for a life full of misery, then we will experience a life full of misery. If we believe that we are worthy of all the good there is to offer then these things will become available to us.

Our thoughts are the most powerful influence we have directing our lives. And our thoughts direct us toward the ultimate outcome – our life experience. Therefore it is empowering to concentrate on what we can control, and we all have the ability to control our thoughts. Our thought forms create our actions and our actions create our life.

Thought is cause; experience is effect. If we don't like the effects in our life then we need to change how we think and our experience will change.

Our thoughts are truly powerful. Our deeply held beliefs, fears, hopes, worries, desires and our attitudes are all conveyed through our thoughts which become our actions, making up our perceptions of ourselves and this world. We have the ability to guide our thinking in a more positive and powerful way. The only real limits are those which we impose on ourselves.

The power of the mind is greatly underestimated and is the most influential tool in the process of the changing of our lives. We are unaware of how powerful the mind really is and how it can work miracles. We can hypnotise somebody and tell them that we are holding a match to their skin, while actually holding a pen to their skin, yet watch it blister. We can hypnotise somebody and operate on them without them feeling any pain and we give placebo tablets to patients instead of drugs and watch as their disease fades away. We only use about five percent of our mind's capacity. Imagine what we would be capable of when we learn to maximise our mind's potential to one hundred percent. By far the most important healing tool would be an awareness of the enormous capability of our own minds. If and when people believe one hundred percent that they have the ability to do something, they usually do. That is the power of the mind.

Our mind is our steering wheel for life, our control panel, and nobody but ourselves has access to those controls. Our thoughts are unique to us and because everybody has different thoughts, ideas and beliefs, everybody will react to the same situation in a different way. We have the power to change the paradigms that dictate our lives. When we change our mind, reality will follow.

Thoughts and imagination are just ideas – possibilities in consciousness. And everything that we see in this physical world started as an idea; an idea that grew as it was focused on, shared and expressed, until it grew into a physical object.

We literally become what we think about most. Our life becomes what we have imagined and believed in most. And this is how we create our own reality.

The world is our mirror – it enables us to experience in the physical plane whatever we hold as our truth.

When we come to the conclusion that we all live our lives by a set of beliefs that we have acquired throughout our own life history, our individually gathered knowledge and experience, we stop being so defensive when others bestow their differences of opinions onto us. The knowledge that everybody has a different set of beliefs gives us credence to allow their opinions to be expressed without the need to defend our own opinion. We are all our unique person with our individual senses and experiences of the world. We do not need conformity or mediocrity. Acceptance is the knowing that there is no need for conflict over a difference of opinion.

When we think of the world in terms of energy, we realise that nothing in the world is solid. Everything and everybody is a vibrational being.

Consciousness creates physical reality. Our thoughts, desires and intentions are vibrational patterns of information that resonate through the universe as energy. The universe then sends back circumstances, events or relationships that match that signal. We get back in life that which we focus on.

Just as we create our reality by using our thoughts and imagination, we create our dreams. All of our thoughts and ideas are converted into our subconscious mind and they are turned into reality in the world of spirit when we close our eyes at night. There we connect to the one universal mind of spirit. In our dream state we are able to create anything we desire, by simply using the power of thought to make it happen. All we need to do is place the thought into our imagination, feel the reality of it, and it will manifest.

> Be careful what you water your dreams with. Water them with worry and fear and you will produce weeds that choke the life from your dreams. Water them with optimism and solutions and you will cultivate success.
>
> Lao Tzu

This is exactly the same concept as in the physical world, except unlike dreams, we have the illusion of time which produces reality at a much slower pace, which gives us the opportunity to learn how to create the realities which we desire.

> Time is the cushion between the thoughts you think and the realities those thoughts produce. Time gives you space to make mistakes.
>
> Lazaris

Life could be looked upon as a self contained novel. We are all here to play certain characters and parts, and each life has its own theme. And we all have the power to write our own script.

At a higher level of consciousness, before we came into our physical bodies we chose certain themes on which to learn and grow from. Our life themes require personal and spiritual growth. There are certain limitations that we need to overcome in order to develop our personal qualities so that we can make our contribution to the universe.

We chose our bodies, race, culture, parents and background in order to match our certain theme. When we look back to our experiences, our challenges, our joys and hardships and our passions, our recurring theme will be revealed.

Life is just an illusion; a dream in which we all produce, star in and direct our own production. If we don't like how the script is written, we can change it. We choose our own script and we can re-write it at any time. Day by day, moment by moment, we create our own reality.

> All the world's a stage,
> And all the men and women merely players,
> They have their exits and their entrances,
> And one man in his time plays many parts...
>
> Shakespeare: As you like it

A great deal of people feel like their life is being led by a series of random events that happen over which they have no control. As a result they are not in any way empowered to change their own destiny.

We have the power to change our thinking patterns in order to make positive change in our lives. We live our lives according to a set of rules that we have created for ourselves – a set of beliefs that were formulated in early childhood. Our subconscious mind supports our internal perception and accepts it as the truth, and those perceptions about ourselves and life become our beliefs. Our lives then start having experiences that revolve around these limiting beliefs and until we change and update those beliefs, we will carry on doing the same thing, saying the same thing and having the same experiences.

Every experience we have had up to this moment was created through a thought or a belief that we had about the past. Every thought and belief that we are having now is creating our future. Our current internal mental dialogue is creating our future. The point of power is always in the present moment, so we need to be very aware of what we are thinking and believing in this very moment.

> What we are today comes from the thoughts of yesterday and our present thoughts build our life of tomorrow. Our life is the creation of our mind.
>
> Buddha

We have the choice to react to our life experiences in fear or love.

A Course in Miracles defines a miracle to be "A shift in perception from fear to love".

The experience that translates everything is within the mind.

When we realise that we have the power to create our own reality through our thoughts we realise that we can experience true happiness and freedom. We realise that WE have the power to give meaning to anything in our world, nothing has any meaning until WE assign a meaning to it, our experience of the world is what WE say it will be, and we are who WE say we are.

> By believing passionately in something that does not yet exist, we create it. The non existent is whatever we have not yet sufficiently desired.
>
> Nikos Kazantzakis

Our creator gave us the power of free will – the freedom to choose how we will think and act.

We are all responsible for our own life experiences.

Nobody can make us feel inferior without our own consent.

As you think – so shall you be. So think only what you want to experience, say only what you choose to make real and do only what you choose to demonstrate as your highest reality.

In every moment we have the choice to create anew.

We have the power to choose our own perceptions, and we have that choice in every single thought that we have.

Our perception then becomes our reality. Confident thoughts create confident people. Timid thoughts create timid people. Loving thoughts create loving people and successful thoughts create successful people.

> Each person experiences a unique reality, different from any other individual's. This reality springs outward from the inner landscape of thoughts, feelings, expectations and beliefs.
>
> Seth

We are responsible for creating our own self image and we are responsible for maintaining it. We have the power to transform our mind.

The mind is a creature of habit and so what dominates the mind, becomes our reality. Therefore it is our responsibility to ensure that our positive thoughts thoroughly influence and outweigh our negative thoughts if we want our outcome to be in spirit.

> Watch your thoughts
> Your thoughts become words
> Watch your words – they become actions
> Watch your actions – they become habits
> Watch your habits – they become character
> Watch your character – for it becomes our destiny.
>
> Lao Tzu

The beauty of creation surrounds us. Every breath that we take, and every word that we speak, and every action and gesture that we make, is forming our lives and our universe. We form the world that we live in, our lives and our experiences. Everything that we do, think and say creates our life story which is that story that we live by. We are continually creating and re-creating our own world and it is profoundly helpful to our spiritual development to review our lives at regular intervals. We need to see how we have adapted to the influences along the way. We have the ability to change, adapt, simplify or entirely change the way we live our lives. We are the co-creators of our lives. As individuals we don't just create our own reality but together with our fellow human beings we co-create the entire world – what we see and experience as real life all around us becomes our reality. Once we begin to understand how this works we can take responsibility for the words, actions and experiences that we produce.

> Each morning we are born again. What we do today is what matters most.
>
> Buddha

Chapter four
TRANSCENDING THE EGO

Transcending the ego is the only way to advance toward the greatest vision that the universe has for us. Ego is what fights with us and stands in our way and if we let it, has the power to keep us from ever becoming our best selves by completely withholding our true spirit. Ego is fear and every time we give in to fear we lose a little bit more power and it begins to take over our lives. Transforming the ego is to take back the power of our true selves – our true spirits. When we transcend the ego we live without fear.

We can wait until nature disintegrates and disperses our bodies and we are transported back to spirit, or through self transformation we can experience spirit in this lifetime.

The belief in "I'm not good enough" is the ego's greatest addiction.

This is the most difficult transformation to make as we have had to continually heed the negative voice of the ego; therefore most of us possess the "I am not good enough" belief. The ego is the fault finder – spirit seeks out innocence.

A major step in transcending the ego is the ability to be able to become conscious of it; to be able to distinguish the ego's voice from that of spirit, and recognise it for what it is – a misguided attempt to bring us down. We need to stay in spirit and then we need to change our thoughts. When we can recognise ego as an illusion of reality it will dissipate. Ego's survival depends on us mistaking it for reality. It is the realisation of who we ARE NOT that the reality of who WE ARE emerges.

We need to recognise that we are all spiritual beings and every time we associate our essence of our being with the ego's self sabotaging voice, the result is the cause of all of our root pain.

The solution is to release that limiting negative belief; free ourselves from the compulsive thinking of the ego and seek a conscious connection to spirit. One of the biggest lessons our souls are put here to conquer is to transcend fear or ego. The soul grows by learning to overcome negative emotions connected to fear by replacing fear with love.

Awareness of the ego is concealed within the present moment. By being present in the moment of now we can transcend the ego. The ego is completely conditioned by the past and the future, so by living in the present moment we can be assured that ego is limited.

The first thing we must do is challenge the ego's voice. We must recognise that the ego's voice was integrated through limited childhood beliefs very early on in our lives, so we are probably carrying around some very outdated beliefs. We need to ask ourselves WHO is really thinking, where did this belief originate from and is it relevant in our lives today. The ego has developed a pattern of behaviour to cope with unmet emotional needs.

The ego always acts in accordance with fear resulting in anger, hostility, a desire to manipulate the situation and insecurity. When others approach us in anger it can become challenging not to let our own ego take control and repel. We then magnify that anger, become defensive and make the situation worse. When we remember that underneath all anger there is pain we will realise that there is something that we need to heal. The pain that has been activated in ourselves is most likely tied to an old wound or weakness in self esteem. It can be a gift in disguise to show us how or where we have been hurt in the past and that we need to work through it. We need to heal the old pain and release the old patterns and find love for ourselves in our own lives. Every situation is an opportunity to gain deep insight and healing. When our pain is activated, instead of responding in anger, we can use the opportunity to find out what negative emotions we have stored in our selves. Spirit reminds us not to take situations and experiences personally and not to act defensively. We may have accepted a negative belief about ourselves by seeing another person's behaviour as a personal attack or insult to us. Other's actions often have little to do with us and more to do with their own pain. It is often ego's feeling of worthlessness, insecurity or abandonment that cause us to feel damaged by others. Most often these events can activate our old belief patterns and perceptions that have been learned early on in life. When we are aware that our reactions to others are based on old belief patterns and pain, we can begin to heal those worn out beliefs. Ego's response therefore can be transcended and spirit can replace anger with love, healing and peace.

Lord make me an instrument of your peace – the first line of the poem by Saint Francis of Assisi.

When we live in spirit we live in peace. We refuse to let our egos or other's negativity bring us down. We refuse to acknowledge their personal complaints and refuse to let them affect our sense of peace. When we refuse to become angry, frustrated or defensive over other people's negativity, we express the universal intelligence within. When we realise that the universal intelligence is in all things, we will know that peace is an expression of universal intelligence and to descend to anger, frustration and defensiveness is to allow the ego to take over. When we transcend the ego we make a conscious decision to transcend negativity. In peace negativity does not exist. When we live in spirit peace will become our lives' predominant experience.

> Lord, make me an instrument of your peace. Where there is hatred, let me sow love; where there is injury, pardon; where there is doubt, faith; where there is despair, hope; where there is darkness, light; where there is sadness, joy.

> O, Divine Master, grant that I may not so much seek to be consoled as to console; to be understood as to understand; to be loved as to love; For it is in giving that we receive; it is in pardoning that we are pardoned; it is in dying that we are born again to eternal life.

Our life's intention is to keep reaching for our highest potential. No matter where we are in this exact place and time we are a single choice away from a new beginning – a new beginning that could impel us to our best possible potential.

> The purpose of your life is to create yourself anew in the next greatest version of the greatest vision ever you held about who you are.
>
> Neale Donald Walsh

We have by now probably come to the conclusion that we have been carrying around ego's limiting beliefs for most of our lives when they should have remained right where they were created – in our childhood.

Now we know how powerful and influential ego has been in our life and we know that we need to choose the positive over the negative in order to be close to spirit.

When we become aware of our ego it automatically begins to dissolve, leaving a feeling of freedom.

We need to replace ego's original thought with the truth as we know it. We need to regularly reinforce our self image with positive, uplifting, inspirational thoughts about ourselves. Introduce these new ideas as affirmations and keep repeating them until they they begin to imprint in our mind. I AM worthy, or I am loveable, will soon become our new belief.

How to help fight the inner critical voice – the ego.

1. Recognise that it is ego's thought and its intentions are to make us feel unworthy.
2. Think about how we feel when we believe that thought to be true.
3. Think about how absurd and untrue that statement really is.
4. Release the thought. We know it is incorrect.
5. Replace the thought with the truth from spirit – a loving heartfelt thought.

> Evil naturally crumbles away when you pay no attention to it.
>
> Lao Tzu

To truly accept the self, we have to change our perceptions of our self. We have the power to change our belief system and start challenging the ego's self sabotaging voice. We have to stop listening to the ego and believe that we are Godlike – we must be like what we came from.

It is a lie to think that you are not good enough. It is a lie to think that you are unloveable.

When we come to the realisation that the negative voices we have been listening to, and the sabotaging advice we have been heeding – thus living our lives by – are a complete and utter lie, a feeling of relief washes over us, bringing a feeling of liberation and freedom. Remember – life is not as serious as the ego makes it out to be!

> The true value of a human being is determined primarily by the measure and the sense in which he has attained liberation from the self.
>
> Albert Einstein

Carl Jung, the psychologist who developed analytical psychology, believed that the object of our lives is to move from ego conscious to the self through individualisation.

Thinking without awareness of the ego is the main component for achieving happiness in our life. Its survival depends on us mistaking it for reality. The recognition of the ego and awareness of spirit is what will ultimately change the direction of our lives.

Freedom from the ego comes from our response to the conditions of our lives.

> Ego says "Once everything falls into place, I will feel peace". Spirit says, "Find your peace and then everything will fall into place".
>
> Marianne Williamson

When we feel resentment we feel bitter, indignant, aggravated and offended. This is our ego reacting. Not reacting to the ego in others is the most effective way of transcending the ego. When we realise and accept that their behaviour as coming from their ego, their false self, we can take comfort in the fact that it is not personal and therefore not become defensive. Resentment occurs when we personalise the actions of the ego. Awareness of the ego erodes the ego. When we can realise and see the ego for what it really is – the negative aspect of the human mind – we will no longer perceive it as other's identity and no longer feel the need to become defensive and angry. When we recognise the false self is at work we can begin to see ourselves beyond our ego to our true selves – our spirit. It will become easier to not react to the ego. The ego thrives on reactivity. Therefore the blaming, judging and complaining will cease and compassion will emerge when we realise that we are all victims of the ego. When we recognise the ego as the illusion that it is, it will dissipate. The recognition of the ego will be the beginning of the transcendence. In seeing that we are not our egos, our true spirit self will emerge.

> After the ego has perished,
> the true self rises from its dust
> like desert flowers
> after spring showers
> have swept across arid plains.
>
> (The Tao is Tao, 21)

Chapter five
UNIVERSAL LAWS

Everything in the universe is made up of atoms. Atoms are energy and everything that exists is made up of energy. Human beings are energy. We think sixty to seventy thousand thoughts every day and these thought processes generate electrical impulses. The brain and the heart produce electrical fields and also produce magnetic fields. Therefore we are powerful magnetic and electrical beings creating energy fields around us and these fields influence every situation or experience in our lives.

On an unconscious level, there is a constant exchange of energy between ourselves, the environment and the people we associate with. We live in a sea of energy and our navigation tools are our thoughts and feelings. Camillo Loken likens ourselves to a sailing ship where the boat is our body, our thoughts are the mast and the wind that blows us to our destination are our feelings. In order to reach our destination, they all must co exist.

When our thoughts and feelings work together, the possibilities are endless. The secret to success is all about our energy, frequency and vibration. The universe is run by certain universal laws and knowing these laws is knowing the rules to the game that we call life.

Transcending the ego requires that we live according to a strong philosophy based on the laws of the universe and our beliefs in the language of the universe.

Trusting in our spirituality is an ally in confronting the ego. The ego is nothing but a misunderstanding of what is real. Our sense of knowing what is true for us will support our ability to transcend the ego. When we trust that we can live a spirit guided life, we can live with peace in our hearts. Once that trust is attained and cemented firmly within us, we know that ego cannot break through that safety chain of truth, for the truth will always be stronger. The universe is so powerful in its positivity that it can withstand all the rigours and tests that ego will place upon us. Only then can we find ourselves living a peaceful, fulfilled, happy, spirit based life.

The law of attraction

The law of attraction is the basis for the following universal laws or hermetic principles. The law of attraction demonstrates how we create the objects, people and events that come into our lives.

The law of attraction is the law by which thought correlates with its object.

An established belief always begins as a thought and is then intensified by an emotion which determines the belief (or disbelief).

The combination of belief, thought and emotion creates an energy which attracts similar energy which is then manifested in the physical world.

Our thoughts, feelings, words and actions all create the energy we send into the universe. Negative energies will always attract negative energies and positive energies will always attract positive energies. It does not matter whether we want the negative outcome or not – what we place our attention on is what we will attract into our life.

A creative force exists that attracts our thought vibrations together that are congruent with like vibrational frequencies to form into physical being, and determines our life experiences based on that which was originally thought.

In order to experience what we "perceive" to be the positive aspects of life, we must first harmonise our thought vibrations with the vibrations of that which we seek to attract.

As you think – so shall you be.

Our experiences in the physical world are a direct result of what we "believe" to be true – whether at a conscious or subconscious level. Our perceptions of ourselves and the world are made up from our core beliefs, thoughts and experiences of our lives and we will attract to ourselves exactly what we believe to be true.

Our physical world is determined by our inner world or thought process (mental or spiritual). Our outside physical world is a direct manifestation of our inner consciousness or thoughts. The quality and consistency of our thinking is the cause of our external circumstances. What those thoughts attract and produce in our lives are the effects that we see.

Resistance is a key factor in the law of attraction.

Focusing on any negative as we think about what we want is resistance. When we put our focus on what we don't want, we will attract into our lives that which we don't want. We need to change our point of attraction from what we don't want to what we do want.

Resistance can come in the form of underlying emotions: Fear, doubts, memories of past failures, etc. We may not be aware that we have these feelings if they are subtle or subconscious.

So we come to the conclusion that we are responsible for the conditions and circumstances of our lives. Life is not determined by fate or chance. The law of attraction delivers to us precisely what we ask it to. If we change our thoughts, we will change our world.

> The most important decision we make is whether we believe we live in a friendly or hostile universe.
>
> Albert Einstein

The law of divine oneness

This law is also called the law of mentalism. It helps us understand that in this universe, we are all connected. There is no separation since everything in the universe, including us, originates from the one source and we will return to the same source. Everything that we see in this physical world has its origin in the invisible realm. There is a single universal consciousness – the universal mind from which all energy and matter are created. Our mind is connected to the universal mind. We are all one infinite, living mind. All creation exists in the mind of spirit and by extension our lives exist in our minds. Therefore spirit is all creation – the universe is a mental creation of spirit.

We live in a world of our own conscious creation.

The law of mentalism ensures that whatever humans have created is the result of their mind. Creation by human beings happens at the mental level and then transforms into the physical. Mind is the seed of creation. The quality of our mind and mental health will, and is determining what type of reality we are experiencing.

All the thoughts, emotions, perceptions, beliefs and imaginations are the products of our mind.

Mind creates matter. The material universe is a universe of mind matter. This mind matter permeates the entire universe, visible and invisible. When we align our mind to mind matter – i.e. "you put your mind to it" – it will materialise because the mind and whatever it is creating are the same matter.

Every condition, every event and experience started out as an idea in the mind. It was by thinking thoughts in the mind that these ideas came into visible manifestation. This is the process of creation.

We can create anything that we put our minds to. There are no limitations.

In the universal sense, there are infinite possibilities because the mind is infinite.

Therefore, so this law states, the mental nature of our existence is that we are all one universal mind. Everything that exists including energy and matter come from this source. We are all an integral part of this universal mind. So when we create our reality, we are not only using our mind but the power of the universal mind. We are all part of spirit's mind because we are all spirit.

Therefore there is no reality; only perception. Our reality is a manifestation of our mind. All things are to our consciousness what we think or believe them to be.

Because we are all living as one universal mind, every thought, action and belief we have, will have a corresponding impact on others and the universe around us.

This law could be called the law of universal intelligence. The universe is this immense world of form in which we find ourselves thinking and breathing. It is about having faith in the universal intelligence that beats our hearts, causes buds to open into blossoms, grows a foetus into a baby, causes a chick to break its shell and all the other incredible miracles that we overlook every day.

By understanding this universal law we can free ourselves from fear and feel safe in the knowledge that spirit is always with us, always guiding us and watching out for us. We just need to open our hearts and listen to the guidance that has always, and will always be there for each and every one of us.

It is the core of living a life with infinite wisdom; knowing how to become in harmony with these laws is the highest level of knowledge that is present in the universe today.

The law of correspondence

The law of correspondence literally tells us that our outer world is a direct reflection of our inner world.

This principle states that our current reality is a mirror of what is happening inside us. If our outer reality is unhappy, fearful or guilty, it is a direct result of what is happening inside us. If we have low self esteem, feel badly about ourselves or constantly feel anger, hatred or blame, then our outer world will be a place of turmoil.

This becomes a continuous cycle – we feel badly about ourselves and our outer world becomes unhappy. The worse the outer world becomes, the worse we feel about ourselves, which has a direct impact on our reality. To escape from this circuit, it is critical to shift our perspective.

Nothing in our outer lives can change without first making changes on the inside. The basis for all self-help is "change from the inside out". It does not matter what we change on the outside, if we haven't done the work to change on the inside. Our reality will continue to evolve so that it is a reflection of our inner beliefs and world.

In all cases, our outer world reflects our inner world in every way, shape and form. If we desire change in our outer world, we must first change our inner world – our thoughts, beliefs and attitudes. Our current situation is a direct result of the way we think. If we want to shift our perception, then we must take responsibility for everything that is happening in our lives and change the way we think.

Our thoughts, feelings and perceptions – what we think internally, are reflected externally. So if you feel that you are unworthy internally then this is what you will reflect externally. If we send out thoughts of fear and separation, then the universe will send those back as catalysts for us to awaken. Our energy will project our perception of ourselves and people will pick up on our vibration that we are not worthy. It is the law of attraction working – this is what we attract to ourselves– what we feel on the inside, we will attract on the outside.

We have total and complete control over only one thing in life: Our thinking. It is not until we change our thought patterns to focus on what it is we truly desire, that we can effect meaningful and lasting change. We have to take responsibility for our own lives and learn to control our own minds. When we succeed in doing this, we take control over all other aspects of our life. This is the key to personal happiness, freedom and peace of mind. By focusing exclusively on what it is that we truly desire, and by eliminating all thoughts of what we don't want, we can begin to shape, mould and build our lives to our own specifications.

> Music in the soul can be heard by the universe.
>
> Lao Tzu

The law of relativity

The law of relativity is relative to all the other laws and states that nothing can be good or bad, big or small until we relate it to something.

The law of relativity tells us that everything in our physical world is only made real by its relationship or comparison to something. Light only exists because we can compare it to dark. Good can only exist because we compare it to bad. Hot can only exist because we can compare it to cold. The quality and value of something can only be measured in relation to another object.

All things are relative. There is no fast or slow, except by comparison. Everything just IS until we compare it to something. Nothing in life has any meaning except the meaning that we give it. It is all in how we look at our situation and what thoughts and perspectives we choose to think about the situation that we arrive at our conclusion. Therefore, whatever we choose to compare things to will determine if we perceive it as good or bad.

Think about the saying, "I once felt bad that I had no shoes – until I met a man who had no feet".

Everything in life is just relative and it is we who decide what value we put on it. It is all in how we relate to everything in our world.

When we relate our experience to somebody else, it will either look more positive or more negative, depending on our perceptions and the labels that we place upon them. If we compare our situation to somebody who is in a considerably less fortunate situation than we are, our situation will always look superior. If we compare our situation to somebody who is in a considerably more fortunate situation that we are, then our situation will always look inferior. No matter what the situation is, there is always going to be somebody more fortunate or less fortunate than we are.

The law of relativity states that all things are relative. We make it what it is.

The law of relativity can be applied to everyday life. Observing our comparisons can either be empowering and uplifting, or self defeating; it is the comparison we make and how we perceive it to be. It is the meaning that WE give to it. We have the choice about what those perceptions are and we have the power to change them. When we change our thoughts and perceptions our lives will change.

When we relate ourselves to others who may be more proficient at something, we put ourselves down and label ourselves as inferior. This is using the law against ourselves.

When this law is properly used, it is to our advantage. We need to be diligent in what we compare ourselves and our situations to. If we constantly compare ourselves to situations that are less fortunate than ours, then we will find all the positives that exist in our life and be thankful, then feel gratitude for all that we already have.

We need to relate to people or situations that bring us joy and heighten our self esteem. Only then in the light of truth will we become aware of how special we really are.

Nothing in life has any meaning, except for the meaning that we give it so we need to make sure that our thoughts and perceptions are in alignment and in resonance with spirit, thus allowing us to lead happy, fulfilled, joyous lives.

> When I let go of what I am I become what I might be.
>
> Lao Tzu

The law of polarity

The law of polarity was created to enable each of us to experience life in its greatest magnificence.

The law of polarity states that everything is on a continuum and has an opposite. There has to be darkness so that we can appreciate the light. Failure exists so that we are aware of what success feels like. Bad experiences exist so that we are aware of what a good experience feels like. There is solid and liquid so that we can see and feel the difference. And of course there is ego and spirit.

We have the ability to suppress and transform undesirable thoughts by focusing on the opposite thought. For example: Negative to positive or hate to love; thereby establishing the desired positive change.

The law of polarity exists as a means to enable us to learn and discover that within every perceived difficulty lies its solution; within every perceived failure lies its success.

The law of polarity contains a vast spectrum of possibilities ranging from the brightest light to the darkest dark. It is our choice, therefore our personal responsibility for whichever end of the spectrum of polarity that we are experiencing.

Within any experience lies the opportunity to experience the opposite. The only thing that determines the outcome, is our choice. What we believe to be true will be the determining factor in our choice as to what end of the spectrum we place ourselves.

By understanding the law of polarity we can learn to fully accept whatever situation arises within our lives without judging it negatively. With that in mind we have the potential to experience harmony and fulfillment in every area of our lives.

> Within the darkest of life's perceived trials and hardships lies the means as well as the ability to find and experience the light.
>
> Chuck Danes

The law of cause and effect

The law of cause and effect states that absolutely everything happens for a reason.

Nothing happens by chance or outside the universal laws. Every action, even thought, has a reaction or consequence and that reaction is always in exact accordance with the action. "We reap what we sow".

The most important lesson involving human conduct and interaction is seen in the law of cause and effect. "For every action there is an equal and opposite reaction". Every human thought, word or decision we make becomes the cause and that gets sent out as energy into the universe, which in turn creates the effect, or the result – whether desirable or undesirable.

Everything that we are and have in our current life is an effect or a result of a specific cause. These causes are the decisions we make and the actions we take on a daily basis. When we choose the behaviour, we choose the consequence.

Our thoughts, behaviours and actions create specific effects that manifest and create our lives as we know it. What we attract is a direct result of the cause that we brought forth into existence.

If we want to change these effects then we must change the cause. If we change our actions we can change our lives. If we transform our thoughts we can create a brand new destiny.

This means that we have to take responsibility for everything that happens in our lives. We can fully realise that success is not created from luck or from something external to us. Success is created from within.

> If you would take, you first must give. This is the beginning of intelligence.
>
> Lao Tzu

The law of vibration

Just as a pebble created vibrations that appear as ripples, which travel outward in a body of water, our thoughts create vibrations that travel outward into the universe, and attract similar vibrations that manifest as circumstances in our lives.

The world of quantum physics has proven that the physical world is one large mass of energy that flashes in and out of being in milliseconds, over and over again.

Everything that we experience through our five senses is conveyed through vibrations. Thoughts, feeling and desires are all vibrations.

Thoughts are what put together and hold together this ever changing energy field into the objects that we see.

Every sound, object and thought has its own vibrational frequency, unique to itself. Negative thoughts create low vibrations and positive thoughts have a much higher vibration.

Unconditional love is the highest of the emotional vibrations and hate is the densest and lowest.

Our bodies are made up of tissues and organs, then cells, then molecules, then atoms, then sub-atomic atoms, and then energy. We are all pure energy light in its most intelligent configuration. It is constantly changing beneath the surface and we can control it all with the power of our mind.

Everything in the universe moves, vibrates and travels in circular patterns.

Nothing is solid. Everything that appears solid is the frequency of the vibration of the energy which makes it up. The higher the frequency, the more potent the force will be. The lower the density of an object, the lower the speed of the vibration. We are pure energy, and everything in the universe is vibrating at different frequencies. If the rate of that vibration falls below or rises above a certain intensity, it becomes invisible to the human senses. Our vibrational frequency is different from other objects in the universe, hence it seems like we are separate from what we see around us – i.e. plants and animals, but we are not separate. We are in fact living in an ocean of energy. We are all connected at the lowest level; this is called the unified field.

Our bodies are made up of ninety percent water and can be programmed and moulded to a certain vibrational frequency via thoughts, sound, colour and love. When we understand how the law of vibration works, we can conceptualise how alternative and holistic treatments can cure the body by changing the vibration of our physical bodies.

Everything begins with a thought. A thought is as real and alive as a rock. Thoughts are communicated by waves or vibrations. The physical materialisation of thought takes form in words. Thoughts are powerful beyond measure. Thoughts are like the ripples flowing outward in a pond when you throw in a pebble. They emanate outwards and resonate in the minds of others. When someone transmits positive and loving thoughts, these thoughts are received by others and produce similar thoughts of love. A thought is a living thing. There is a strength and a power in a thought, and we must learn to use them wisely. Whatever we focus our mind on we will create. When we change our thoughts, we change our lives. With our thoughts we can either build or destroy.

Our thoughts and feelings in the present moment dictate our dominant vibration. Thoughts and feelings are what we use to define conscious awareness of vibration and our thought is considered to be the highest form of vibration, therefore it has the highest frequency. It is considered as a powerful force in the universe and we are continuously transmitting our thoughts and feelings into the universe.

If we choose to think positive thoughts we will attract positive vibrations. If we choose to think negative thoughts, we will attract negative vibrations. Feelings of love, joy and gratitude have a faster vibration than fear, grief or despair. Our thoughts will always resonate in vibrational harmony with other corresponding vibrations.

Everything is linked to energy, vibration and frequency. All of our negative energy is draining to our universe. People who live in constant fear emit the most negative energy and it is the cumulative effect of so many negative thoughts that is contributing to many of the world's problems. When we learn to live from spirit the level of energy on earth would change from the lower frequency of fear to the higher frequency of unconditional love. Communication with spirit thus becomes easier.

Knowing this universal law we can all allow ourselves to consistently attract the desired events, conditions and circumstances of our lives. We can create our own life experiences.

The law of rhythm

This law tells us that there is always a reaction to every action. Something must advance when anything retreats; something must rise when anything sinks.

Everything vibrates and moves to certain rhythms. These rhythms establish seasons, cycles and stages of development and patterns in the universe. Nature is a rhythm. We have seasons, days, cycles, minutes, earth, sky, the sun and the moon all working together to help create this wonderful universe that we live in.

Each cycle reflects the regularity of the universe. This is evident in the ebbs and flow of the tides of the ocean, the rising and setting of the sun and moon and in the swaying of our thoughts from positive to negative.

This law states that everything is moving to and fro, flowing in and out, swinging backward and forward. There is a high and a low tide, therefore we will not always feel emotionally or physically the same from one day to the next. Just as the universe has cycles, so do our bodies. Our negative feelings are what permit us to feel our positive feelings.

A new cycle begins every day, every moment. So if we need to recognise anything, let it be what that symbolises; the miracle of the endlessly continuing cycle of life.

> Only if you have been in the deepest valley, can you ever
> know how magnificent it is to be on the highest mountain.
> Richard Nixon

There will always be highs and lows in life. We have the ability to choose our thoughts because we are born with free will. We can decide what to think any moment of our lives. Even when we are on a natural down swing, we can choose good thoughts with our free will and continue to move up toward our goals.

> To permit your mind to dwell upon the inferior is to
> become inferior and to surround yourself with inferior
> things. On the other hand, to fix your attention on the
> best is to surround yourself with the best, and to become
> the best.
> Bob Proctor

To be fully aligned in spirit we must accept and understand that the universe was created with great magnificence.

Think about the changes in season – in autumn the leaves fall to the ground. During winter those leaves decompose and fertilise the soil. In spring the warm air and fertilised soil makes perfect conditions for bulbs and seeds to grow. Then in summer those flowers bloom for all to enjoy.

All people have within them the power to change the conditions of their lives. We are the creators of our own lives. What we believe about ourselves will come true. We all have the ability to change the way we think and if we change our thoughts we can transform our lives.

How we conduct ourselves along the path that is our life determines how our life unfolds. Higher vibrations consume and transform lower vibrations, thus each one of us can change the energies in our lives by understanding the universal laws and applying the principles in such a way as to create positive change.

The law of growth (creation)

Everything in this universe has a beginning or creation. Everything that manifests in the world of shape and form must begin as a seed – humans, plants, animals, thoughts, illnesses, disease, experiences, events, situations and circumstances.

Everything that is in this physical realm, whether it be in nature or in our personal lives, is always the result of spirit. The law of growth ensures that the seeds that we have planted will grow into materialisation.

The law of growth states that for every seed planted a harvest will be received. Or that for every cause there must be an equal effect.

The power of our thoughts represent the seeds that we choose to plant into the spirit realm. Infinite intelligence will then ensure that a consequence is produced based on the variety and quality of the thought. Spirit and plants are alike in that they both lean toward the light.

The law of growth fundamentally determines our life experience, founded by the affirmation that says once the seed has been planted something must grow. The outcome will be dependent on the variety and quality of the seed initially planted.

Therefore we must ask ourselves if we are consciously aware of the quality of the seed which we are planting.

Once the seed is planted the law of growth (or creation) which is intrinsically connected to, and works in perfect harmony with all the other universal laws will with absolute certainty guarantee that new life is inevitable.

Just like in nature a seed must first be sown to determine what the harvest will be. Based on the variety and quality of the seed planted the harvest will produce a corresponding outcome. All that can grow is based on the seeds that are provided to grow. The law of growth doesn't judge or make determinations as to what is grown but can only operate within the constraints of its intended purpose.

The law of growth allows us to understand how it is that the events, conditions and circumstances that we experience in our life come into being. Doing so will enable us to better understand and see the crucial nature of becoming and remaining consciously aware of the seeds that we are planting which determine our consequences.

Understanding the law of growth and how it operates in its unwavering and predictable nature can allow us to plant, with certainty and conscious intention, the desired ideas and thoughts which in turn will produce the desired effects.

The thought seeds nurtured by emotions of doubt, anxiety, fear, lack and discord will only produce outcomes in the physical world that are of the same variety and quality of the seed planted. Once sown, we can be certain that this harvest must grow. This enables and empowers us to become detached from the outcome, for we know that through the process of creation, we will receive in exact correlation with what is asked. When we plant thought seeds of love, honesty, gratitude and happiness, they are the values that we will ultimately grow into our lives.

When we plant thought seeds of doubt and fear, they are the concepts that we will ultimately grow into our lives.

We have the ability to consciously plant 60,000 thought seeds every single day. We need to learn to place conscious awareness on the variety and quality of what we are projecting out into the field of infinite potentiality.

When we become aware of how the law of growth (creation) operates, we realise that we have the power to create any physical, mental or spiritual outcome that we desire. We will come to know what it means to become a conscious and purposeful creator of the events, conditions and circumstance that make up our life experience.

Whatever we are experiencing in our life, whether it is a desirable outcome or a less than desirable outcome, we must realise that we are responsible for the relevant consequences.

The law of growth in its predictable certainty guarantees that the thought intention of the seed that we plant into the realm of spirit will manifest into our experiences and the conditions of our lives. When we can consciously select the thought seeds that we intend to manifest, we can produce the desired result and we will soon know what it means to experience a life filled with love, joy, fulfillment, contentment and inner peace in each and every area of our life.

The law of perpetual transmutation of energy

The law of perpetual transmutation of energy states that all of us have within us the power to change the conditions of our own lives. Higher vibrations consume and transform lower vibrations; therefore each of us can change the energies in our lives by understanding the universal laws and applying the principles in such a way as to effect change.

We are never perplexed, no matter the circumstance of our lives. The universe always allows us the opportunity to grow and evolve and is constantly giving us opportunities to do so. All we have to do is raise our vibration and take action.

The law of perpetual transformation of energy or the law of energy says that all energy is in a constant state of motion and that all energy that is in motion will eventually appear in the physical form. Therefore energy forms into thought.

This universal law states that whatever we spend our time thinking about, whatever we dwell on, whatever we worry about, will eventually appear in the physical form.

This law relates to the universe and our consciousness through the realisation that everything seen and unseen is constantly transmuting or changing. It is the cause and effect of itself and to resist change is to go against this universal law. We ourselves are in constant transmutation; to change is to grow and if we resist growth and change then we resist the pathway of life.

In his book, "The Science Of Getting Rich," author Wallace D. Wattles talks about the law of perpetual transmutation. Simply put, energy from the formless realm is constantly flowing into the material world and taking form. This energy is limitless and inexhaustible. As old forms are exhausted, they give way for new forms to emerge from the invisible hidden energy of the universe.

Thoughts are energy and we can transmute or change our energy. We can change our energy from one form to another; therefore we can change our thoughts.

To change an energy from one form to another, we just change that thought that created the energy that was initially created.

We created the initial thought within our mind. We can just as easily change our thoughts by bringing into our minds a new form of energy. This law of the transmutation of thought into the physical form is strongest when our thoughts are consistent. The most prevalent energy will always dominate.

The world that we live in is a huge mass of energy created by everybody and everything and we are affected by our environment which is that energy.

Change begins with each of us. Thus, as we begin to change our negative thoughts, we affect others. Our energy affects all those surrounding us.

As we stay balanced within ourselves and maintain a happy feeling inside, that feeling will be reflected on the outside. Everybody and everything that comes into contact with our happy energy will be affected in a positive way.

Our minds are very powerful and because of this, the mind will discard any thought that is not important, or random, or thoughts that are not congruent with our personal beliefs.

The law of perpetual transmutation of energy responds to the most dominant thoughts in our minds. The thoughts our minds considered to be important are those thoughts that are consistent. When we worry, the prevalent thoughts in our mind are with that of which we are worried about, so those thoughts will be the most dominant, therefore those are the thoughts that are manifested.

If we are not happy with what we are manifesting, then it is up to us to change our dominant thoughts to those things that we do want. Instead of focusing on the things that we do not want as opposed to the things we do want we will see an extraordinary change in our lives.

Because the law of perpetual transmutation of energy responds to the dominant thoughts in our minds, we need to make sure that the dominant thoughts in our minds are those which we wish to manifest.

The law of energy responds to our thoughts. It cannot differentiate between negative or positive thoughts. It will respond to any thought that is created in our mind. It does not matter if the thought that we are creating is "I am worthy," or, "I am unworthy". The law of energy will respond to the most dominant thought and manifest that into our lives. It is all our choice.

Therefore it is most important to our wellbeing and happiness that we make sure that our thoughts are producing the results we desire in our lives.

Mother Teresa was once asked why she did not participate in anti-war demonstrations. She replied that she never would do that, but as soon as there was a pro-peace rally, she would be there. If we focus on what we want (peace) instead of what we do not want (war) we will receive it in abundance. Let's focus, pray, rally and preach peace and we shall have it. Don't focus on what we don't want. Focus on what we do want.

The law of action

The law of action requires us to take a proactive role in creating our life.

The law of action must be applied in order for us to manifest anything here in the physical plane of existence. There is a time for silence, for vision, and for focused intent. There is also a time for action. We need to decide on what situation or experience we want to have, then take reasonable steps toward those goals. Moving from the realm of imagining, feeling and thinking about the goal to putting it into physical action, or movement toward that goal, is essential for the law of action to succeed. As we take these steps, we will notice that we begin to attract more of what we need to take further action and the further action we take, the more we create what it is that we want.

We have the power to set our intentions about what we want in life and then attract it to ourselves via focused thought. Then with the power of the law of action, when we add momentum, or action to our intentions, we create our physical intentions. Creative action has power beyond what we understand and it will always work to our benefit.

The power of the universal law of action states that each day we are given new opportunities that require our continuous input, choices and actions. We have the choice of whatever intention we want to create by taking action. Therefore we have the ability to create an empowered life, full of whatever it is that we desire. We create our own unique journey.

> If we do not change direction – we may end up where we are heading.
>
> Lao Tzu

The law of compensation

The universal law of compensation states that "We get back what we give to others".

It is a basic understanding that what we project out is returned to us. Like attracts like.

If most of what we send out into the world is positive, most of what we receive in return will also be positive.

When working with the law of compensation we want to give out that which we wish to receive. Therefore if we work to be a strong, nurturing, and supportive person for others, chances are when we are in need of support ourselves we will have this same strength and support returned to us.

We have all heard, for example, the saying "Misery loves company," which highlights this law quite well. When people are angry, hurting, negative and miserable they tend to complain a lot, and that sends out the energy of anger, hurt, negativity and misery, and in return they attract more people or circumstances that return to them the energy that they are projecting.

Ghandi once said we must be the change we wish to see in the world. In other words, rather than whining and complaining about everything that is wrong in our lives – we could take on a positive, empowered stance toward life. We would then find that the world and our perceptions of others will change. We will become more inclined to see the good in ourselves and others.

You have probably noticed that when someone smiles at you, your energy shifts instantly. You are inclined to smile back or say hello. That simple acknowledgment is a great example of how the law of compensation works and is best summed up by the saying "You reap what you sow".

> Everything that irritates us about others can lead us to an understanding of ourselves.
>
> Carl Jung

When we give freely of what we want to see and experience and be what we want to see in the world, those things will be reflected back to us.

When we are generous and proactive it allows more abundance and opportunities to flow into our lives.

When we are miserly and afraid of losing everything, we tend to attract more debt and hardship because that is where we are directing our energy.

We have to know at a conscious level what we want to experience.

Be what you want to be and it will come back to you.

> Knowing others is wisdom, knowing yourself is enlightenment.
>
> Lao Tzu

When we become aware of the universal laws we realise how they all work together in perfect harmony and unity within each other to form this miraculous universe and allow our lives to evolve in the most amazing journey of this gift that we choose to call life. This connection within the universal laws ensures that the cosmos remains balanced and operating within a perfectly constructed process.

Once we begin to incorporate a philosophy into our lives that is in accordance with our universal laws, everything becomes clear. These are deeply philosophical rules for living that require effort and dedication to fully integrate, but once we master them we will see the results in profound ways. It will be truly life altering.

Chapter Six

TEACHERS

When the student is ready – the teachers will appear.

Life is not a destination, but a wonderful journey and we are blessed to have teachers who come in many forms to help guide us along the way.

Our experiences are great teachers. Through our experiences of life, from the time we are born to the time that we die, we are constantly learning and growing physically, mentally and spiritually. We all make mistakes and in reality our mistakes are our greatest teachers.

Knowing that crisis gives way to new opportunities is the ultimate intelligence.

> The basis of life is freedom. The purpose of life is joy. The outcome of life is growth.
>
> Abraham

Out of the darkest and most painful experiences of our lives we will find our deepest healing and most profound healing. When we make mistakes and errors in judgments they offer us insight. In order to learn life's lessons we must make mistakes and when we alter our perception of reality through making mistakes, growth is irrefutable. As we continue to learn and grow we are able to offer our wisdom as a gift that empowers the life of others. Pain, loss, joy and love are all a part of life. Life is fundamentally a continuous growth experience and our life lessons are learned in how we respond to those experiences. Some experiences will ultimately be more enjoyable than others but they are all a part of the curriculum. All of life's lessons revolve around love and fear and every action is either an expression of love or a call for love. Failure is a vital part of achieving success. Our errors of judgments are made to bring us to a point of awareness. The challenging situations that happen in life are spirit's way of sending us into a deeper awareness.

> No one can reach heaven who has not yet passed through hell.
>
> Aurobindo

The purpose of our lives is to re-create ourselves in the most wonderful, exceptional, loving fun way we could ever imagine.

We are all intentional players with respect to how we live, love and learn.

Every soul that chooses to be born into this incarnation will have its own blueprint; encoded within it are all our gifts, talents and abilities as well as the lessons that we need to learn. We choose our life lessons and they include experiences of hardship. The lessons that will make the greatest impact, those which we will remember the most, have a tendency to be the painful ones. The most painful experiences can be a powerful teacher of wisdom and knowledge for our soul. Our gifts, talents and abilities, along with our joys and hurts will make up our true self and help us live a life in full alignment with our purpose. The difficult experiences of life are just as valuable as the joyous ones. We all experience suffering in our lifetimes. No matter what causes the pain it can leave a scar on our soul. We are likely to have one major soul wound and knowing what that is will help us find one of the gifts or talents that we were meant to share with the world. This will always be to help heal someone or something. Once the soul wound has been enabled to heal, it has had a chance to advance and grow. The wound has enhanced the soul and who we have become because of it.

This gives us the perfect opportunity to use this lesson as a gift to assist and heal others. We can use our loss to help change and inspire others. When we use our pain to help others, we heal the wound as well as ourselves. Living with the purpose of aiding and healing others and being all that we can be is a true reflection of our divine source. Our ultimate journey is to learn the lesson, understand what it was meant to teach us, heal and recover from it and go on to help others.

The pain can be healed but it will always leave a scar. Pain does not have to define us but can act as a transformational antidote when applied correctly. When we can learn, honour and grow from our pain we can allow it to become a powerful and motivating source, guiding us toward the next step we take on our journey.

> New beginnings are often disguised as painful endings.
> Lao Tzu

Everything happens to challenge, support or change the way we live our lives. The reason may not be immediately clear, but it has to do with our soul lessons. We each have a soul lesson to learn and it may be that we need to learn a certain lesson before we can move onto the next stage of our spiritual development. When we keep repeating the same patterns, divine intelligence is suggesting that we haven't yet mastered the lesson. The purpose of our lives is to learn; to accomplish that which our souls have chosen as its programme. Each soul has a different programme, therefore no two souls need to learn or accomplish the same thing. The soul's path is to grow and each path is unique to each soul. Some soul lessons could include forgiveness, compassion, self-worth, patience, understanding or unconditional love.

Our life purpose is to learn, grow and move forward. We either learn our lessons or we choose to ignore the lesson, thus we end up repeating the same experiences over and over until we learn from it and change our way of thinking. Our soul's journey is planned according to our life's lessons – the life's lessons that we have not learned from our previous life experiences. Our purpose is to learn and grow from the challenges that we have chosen for ourselves – the challenges that we selected when we sat with our creator to create our life journey before we were born. Once we have learned all of our lessons, we earn our angel wings and we can choose to stay in the spirit realm.

Our free will gives us the power of choice but that can cause hurt and pain. If we keep making the same choice and each time we make that choice, it causes us pain, it is because we haven't yet learned from experience to make a different choice next time. Nobody is punishing us; we are simply punishing ourselves. Divine intelligence is directing us in the direction of change on our spiritual path.

Those people who are in our lives as well as those who have moved on have either been drawn to us or us to them to learn some aspect of our lesson. There are no coincidences. We are all here for a reason, and everything happens for a reason. Every situation and every experience is an integral part of our life's plan and at some stage we will get an opportunity for understanding and insight.

In retrospect, after going through a certain experience, or being in a certain situation, we can look back with the wisdom that comes with hindsight and see that the experience was an important and necessary step in some way toward the consequence of our lives today. Spirit knows that the universe is in a perfect state of balance and that all the circumstances that we find ourselves in have been created entirely by that soul for the purpose of experience. As such we know that the universe is perfectly safe.

> Life will give us whatever experience is most helpful for
> the evolution of our consciousness. How do you know this
> is the experience you need? Because this is the experience
> you are having at this moment.
>
> Eckhart Tolle

We could look at our lives as like a giant jigsaw puzzle. Every illness, chance meeting, accident, event or situation that happens is there is to serve a purpose. All of these things form a piece of the puzzle and eventually we begin to see a bigger picture emerging. There is a master plan in existence – a much bigger picture and we are all here for a purpose.

Every experience we have ever had has taught us something that is essential to our lives today.

We may not arrive at this perspective until a long while after the actual event, but eventually when we look back we are able to see that everything had a purpose and a meaning and we will see that there was a certain lesson that needed to be learned, a deepening of our wisdom, a new awakening, or a new path unfolding which we needed to follow.

> Always be on the lookout for ways to turn a problem into
> an opportunity for success.
>
> Lao Tzu

Life's adventures are only possible because of life's challenges. Divine intelligence is our choreographer, formulating steps in the forms of life experiences that will bring about the lessons that we need to learn. Creating experiences that, as they unfold will seem to have no reason, although in hindsight the perfection will be obvious and the meaning understood.

> Your petty tyrants are your greatest teachers.
>
> Carlos Castenada

We learn nothing from a lifetime filled with happiness. When we think of the most difficult and heart-breaking experiences we have endured in our lives, we can appreciate how much we have really learned from those experiences and how they have shaped us into becoming the person that we are today.

Incarnating into a human body provides a level of learning that cannot be accomplished in any other dimension. If we haven't completed the purpose of our programme in this lifetime, we will continue it when the soul returns at a later date and moves into another human body. There are certain lessons that need to be learned only through living a human existence. The mission of our soul incarnating into human form is to elevate to a higher spiritual level.

The universe is always unfolding exactly as it should. All incidents in our lives have a purpose. Sometimes we may get experiences in the form of peace and serenity, other times our experiences may come in the form of challenge and conflict. Each experience is specifically designed for our own personal evolution. Whether we are in a situation of abundance, or in a situation of poverty, the conditions are uniquely configured to help create who we were supposed to be. The experience or situation that we are having at this moment is the experience or situation that is needed for our personal growth, simply because we are experiencing it now.

Every human being is a work in progress. Any pain, disappointment or chaos that exists in our lives is not because this is how life is meant to be, but only because we have not yet finished the work that brought us here. That work is the process of freeing ourselves from the domination of ego and creating an affinity with the sharing essence of spirit.

Everything happens for a reason, and everything that happens to us is always for our greatest benefit. Every experience that happens to us plays a part in the formation of our character and our fate. Although we are not always aware of it at the time, as a result of that experience that we perceived to be negative at the time, our lives were changed in a dramatically constructive way. Disappointments are a sign from spirit that there are better things to come.

> Failure is an opportunity
> If you blame someone else
> There is no end to the blame
> Therefore the master fulfills her own obligations
> and corrects her own mistakes
> She does what she needs to do
> And demands nothing of others.
>
> Lao Tzu

With this knowledge we can trust in spirit to allow the situation to unfold before we categorise each event in a positive or negative according to how pleasant or convenient it happens to be for us at that particular moment.

We can gracefully accept whatever new experiences, events or situations that come into our lives, no matter what they may be, with the knowledge that there will be a certain lesson, wisdom or opportunity that will arise from it. We can move forward in our lives, knowing that we don't have all the answers but knowing that we will be guided by intuition and faith.

When we trust in the unknown, we realise that there is a mysterious force and rhythm to life that supports and assists us in every way.

When we maintain the perspective of acceptance in all situations, our lives will enter into a new realm of peace and serenity. When we are accepting of all the experiences and trust in the challenges of our lives, it gives us strength to surrender to the calmness and peacefulness of spirit, knowing that we are being guided, looked after and never alone. We are never without opportunities and choices. Trusting in the process of life empowers us to take chances and gives us courage. Trusting in the process of life is the foundation for happiness. When we understand that everything in our lives happens for a reason and everything happens to serve us in some way, we can let go and let God.

Carl Jung – a famous philosopher would tell those friends who reported a tragic event, "Let us open a bottle of wine. Something good will come of this". If his friends reported some wonderful event, he would say, "That's too bad, but if we stick together, maybe we can get you through this".

Wisdom can be found everywhere. The moment that we are willing to make a change in our lives, the universe automatically responds with a tool to help us on the way. When we are gifted with a message we will start to see, hear and feel it in every part of our lives. It may be a book, an online course, a workshop or a conversation with a friend. Every experience that we have is an opportunity to learn and grow. Coincidences are spirit's way of remaining anonymous. Serendipity occurs in our lives as a sign that we are on the right path, therefore if we fail to recognise the messages the first time, they will continue to reappear until we address them. If we perceive everybody who we come into contact with and every experience that we have as an opportunity to learn and grow we will no longer feel the need for anger, resentment or bitterness. There is always a gift or lesson to be found in an affliction or adversity. Afflictions heal and adversity opens us to a new reality, therefore there is wisdom in every wound.

A certain experience may lead to some spiritual or emotional healing, or the opportunity to discover that we need to change the direction of our lives.

When we let go of an old perspective or idea, we open ourselves up to a new idea or perspective with the knowledge that everything and everybody is continually growing and changing. Change means that we free ourselves from feelings of isolation, separation, loneliness, anger, fear and pain. We create lives filled with peace and we can relax and enjoy life as it is and be safe in the knowledge that there is always a consequence for these changes and they are all designed to make our lives more successful, peaceful, happy and fulfilled.

When we look back we will be aware of the forces in our lives that have created these causes and the effects will be completely obvious.

Our spirit is our greatest teacher. Spirit's power is constantly working to provide to us the lessons that we need in order to learn and grow as individuals. Each of us is part of the spiritual class offered for the evolution of the soul. Everywhere; all the time spirit is connecting with us. Not in physical energy, but in the book that beckons you in the library, the workshop pamphlet that is delivered to your letterbox, or the song that is playing on the radio. Spirit is always guiding us for our own benefit. Universal law automatically and instantly sends us a continual stream of opportunities and experiences in order to discover the universal truth about ourselves and the world. We will always attract the perfect lesson, whatever that may be, that suits our current life blockages, desires or questions. We need to recognise that these lessons are sent to us for our highest good and best intentions to help us break free of limiting and ego (fear) based beliefs. If we do not recognise the opportunities for growth and learning then we will continuously be sent these lessons over and over again, in different forms, until we master the lesson. Gratitude is our way of expressing to the universe our thankfulness for these lessons and the fact that we trust in the universal law of cause and effect. We realise that every effect is merely the cause of our thoughts, and all of our situations and experiences were created by our thoughts, thus the need to discover and eradicate the thoughts that we do not want to materialise in our own lives.

All of a sudden we can see clearly, and be grateful for the way that life has unfolded in the way that it has. We can then be grateful for both our friends and our adversaries, and for both the joys and challenges of our lives because the joys give us pleasure and the challenges help us to learn and grow. Everything serves in its own way. We can then relax, feel peace and marvel at the amazing journey that has taken place in our lives. The universal laws are always in effect and it is all just complete perfection.

Ram Dass was said to become depressed after his stroke 10 years before. After all it took him away from his beloved game of golf, his cello and anything else that he could do with his hands. He realised the gift when "grace" forced him from the "distractions" to go deeper and deeper inside himself and explore peace and love.

Wayne Dyer has expressed that his greatest teacher was his father – a drunk uncaring man who left his wife with three small boys. His father taught him forgiveness.

> At the centre of your being you have the answer, you know who you are and you know what you want.
>
> Lao Tzu

Spiritual intuition

We are not human beings having a spiritual experience; we are spiritual beings having a human experience.

There is a universal intelligent life force that exists within everybody and everything. It resides deep within each of us as a deep wisdom, an inner knowing. We can access this source of wisdom through our intuition. Intuition is a deep knowing that the guidance which is the truth is always moving us in the direction of our self development. The intuitive mind has an infinite supply of information, including information that we have not yet gathered directly through personal experience. Spirit can tap into the universal mind at any given moment and be given an endless supply of knowledge and wisdom whenever we need it to help us develop our sense of self.

Spirit guides through the intuitive voice. All we have to do is listen and be aware of its presence.

Spirit is the pure love and divine intelligence that rules the universe and is a part of who we all are. Intuition is the voice of love and inspiration.

Intuition connects us to the divine universal intelligence and helps us to live our lives fully and with joy and purpose.

That voice is coming from the same non physical energy which is growing our fingernails, beating our heart, blossoming the flowers in the springtime when the earth is much warmer and all the other miraculous events taking place in the universe. Through intuition we gain enlightenment and direction from the universal intelligence that surrounds us, internally and externally. It is what makes up our world. It is part of who we are. We cannot see or touch it but we can experience it.

Through our intuition we can receive invaluable information, guidance and direction. Intuition may come in the form of an inner voice, a gut feeling, dreams, sensations, feelings, or thoughts. That voice is spirit and spirit is calling us. It is our free will to choose whether or not to follow that inner calling. That intuition is bringing to us the very ideas, insights and solutions we need in order to fulfill our inquiries while here on this journey on earth. Once we have acquired the ability to listen to and trust this intuition, we realise that we are never alone or without guidance.

We all have a purpose and a mission in life. When we have a deep knowing that our lives are being lived with purpose we will feel joy and enthusiasm. The basis of the word enthusiasm is entheos which literally means "God within". Thus when we feel enthusiastic about our lives, we can know that spirit is speaking within us and guiding us through our intuition.

> Feeling is God's mirror; intuition is God's telephone.
>
> Kenny Loggins

Intuition is spirit's wisdom, guiding us through our lives. It is always giving us an unfailing direction towards our hopes, dreams and life's lessons. When we learn to use the gift of intuition to positively enhance the quality of our lives, we will begin to experience more freedom, joy, satisfaction and happiness from our lives.

Intuition connects us with the universal intelligence within. Our intuition allows us to solve life's most innermost struggles and deliberations when we quiet ourselves enough to listen and be guided. Intuition can provide us with a peaceful outcome in the midst of a seemingly disastrous experience, help us to see a person or experience from a different perspective, provide answers when we have no idea which direction to take, help us to release judgments or take action to prepare us for a change in our lives.

> If prayer is you talking to God then intuition is God talking to you.
>
> Wayne Dyer

Spiritual guidance always acts in accordance with our happiness and fulfillment. The guidance we hear will direct us to our true purpose and meaning. Every time we are guided by our intuition and act on the wisdom that we receive, we align our mind with spirit; divine intelligence.

When we learn to use our inner spirit regularly and trust in its guidance, we can rely on the fact that our intuition is always accurate and therefore modify our perceived belief that we are alone in this world without direction or meaning. Life takes on more of a flowing, effortless quality.

Intuition is a deep sensing and knowing of the truth and a feeling of peace without reasoning or understanding.

Carl Jung calls intuition one of the four basic psychological functions along with thinking, feeling and sensation. He describes it as the function that explores the unknown and senses possibilities and implications which may not be readily apparent.

> God speaks to us every day, only we don't know how to listen.
>
> Mahatma Gandhi

As more of us awaken our powers of intuition through personal growth, human consciousness will be increasingly open to and conditioned by the universal truth – the sense of unity with all that is. The illusion of separateness has always been the greatest single obstacle to human growth. When we are aware of and trusting in the intuition that is providing us the guiding light, our approach to life will become more comprehensive, and we will realise that we have the ability to dispel all of the illusions that ego has manifested. It is through intuition that the illusions disappear. Intuition is the antidote to illusion.

Intuition is a complete expression of the truth, whereas illusion is the complete concealment of truth. Intuition is insight into reality whereas illusions are unrealistic insights into false concepts. Intuition is the experience of identification with the whole whereas illusion distorts this into the sense of identification with parts of the whole.

> Without stirring abroad one can know the whole world; without looking out the window one can see the way of heaven.
>
> Lau Tzu

When we are listening to ego's (fear's) voice, we are restricted by the five physical senses. Ego has an agenda that keeps us limited in our thoughts and our abilities. Nothing in nature is random. Something that appears random is only through the limits of our knowledge. Our fearful ego knows that if we listen to our divine guidance we will no longer be afraid. The ego consists completely of fear so when we lose our fear, the ego loses its existence. Hence ego will keep us from the peace of mind that comes from listening to divine guidance. When we permanently lose our ego, we will lose the fear that isolates us from the peace of mind that keeps us from living the life we were born to live.

> The communication link that God himself placed within you, joining your mind with his, cannot be broken. You may believe you want it broken, but this belief does not interfere with the deep peace in which the sweet and constant communication God would share with you is known. Yet his channels of reaching out cannot be wholly closed and separated by Him.
>
> A Course in Miracles

Spirit informs us of the complete unbiased truth without any distorted information. Spirit will guide us as we explore a new awareness and find our true purpose and identity – that purpose and identity that ego has held a mask over for so long. When we detach from the ego we will discover with immense clarity the meaning of life.

Spirit allows us to accept the fact that we are so much more than our physical body. When we realise that we are spirit and can accept the fact that we are all one divine being, therefore communicating all of the time, we will heed guidance from the spirit voice or intuition. It will eventually become a familiar deity, a beam of light that remains within us at all times that will alter our perceptions and change our reality in a truly miraculous way. Our lives will become everything that we ever wanted – happiness, fulfillment, joy and unconditional love.

> There is a voice that doesn't use words. Listen.
>
> Rumi

Synchronicity

A synchronicity is a meaningful coincidence. It is a sign from the universe, guiding and directing us; helping to align our personal growth. It is a reminder that unknown forces in our universe have the capacity to make the contents of the invisible realm of consciousness visible in the world of form. Synchronicity often happens around a memorable occasion, for example a death in the family. Those of us who are fortunate enough to have been a given a sign from the universe will recognise it as having special meaning to us. While intuition is an internal sign, synchronicity is an external sign.

Synchronicity springs from the deepest form of destiny. Synchronicity is the law of unity. It confirms that we are all connected to spirit. It establishes the reality that there is a higher dimension of consciousness and that there is no separation between matter and spirit; there is no separation between anyone or anything. Everything is connected. Synchronicity is the universal consciousness, the binding force of all life giving us messages of clarity.

Once we are aware of synchronicity, we will begin to see it everywhere. The universe is communicating with us – empowering us to evolve to a higher consciousness. The higher and clearer our frequency, and the more consciously aware we are, the better our ability to decipher synchronicity.

Each day our life encounters meaningful synchronicity and intuition. Souls create synchronicity which are gifts given to us in the physical. In every moment the universe is whispering to us. There is wisdom to be found in every moment, and everyday events in our life carry communications from the realm of spirit. We just have to be open and willing to receive. It is why we are here. That is how our reality works. Synchronicities are messages from divine intelligence guiding us in ways to help us on our journey. They are meaningful life opportunities.

> Every experience of synchronicity is a daring invitation
> to let go of ego long enough to design a destiny in accord
> with the purposes of love.
>
> David Richo

To accept that we are a divine expression of spirit and that divine intelligence is always guiding us through life is to accept that we are souls with unbelievable power. It is a power that is our birthright, yet we often refuse to acknowledge it which prevents us from being all that we can be. Action equals power and when we take one step toward discovering the unlimited potential of our souls, that is the beginning of being all that we can be. We have to realise the relevance of the source's wisdom. Most of the conflict in our lives manifests when we do not act in accordance with our inner guidance. If we are not in alignment with our soul we become very unbalanced.

Divine intelligence has created a perfect example of synchronicity in nature. We see birds that fly in perfect formation with hundreds of other birds. When they change direction they all execute the same motion synchronistically. Each bird will move in harmony with every other bird without an apparent leader. They can change direction in an instant and all birds alter their course at the exact same moment. This means that all of the correlation of activity is internally communicated. Schools of fish use the same instantaneous form of communication. This comes from the non verbal divine intelligence. These examples of synchronicity can be found so often in nature because nature is more in tune with spirit. As humans we have allowed the ego to lose our sense of connection with spirit. Our sense of separation has obscured our connection to divine intelligence. As the earth travels around the sun it creates seasonal rhythms. From winter to spring the birds begin to migrate, flowers bloom, trees bud, fruit ripens and birds hatch. It all acts in unison with each other. All of nature is one – a symphony – and we are a part of that. Synchronicity is the rhythm of life. The cycles all correspond with each other; the seasons, the tides, the sun and the moon and we are a part of the rhythms of life. Divine intelligence is in us and around us. It is spirit from which everything emerges. We are all one. Divine intelligence is the soul of all things. We are connected to the rhythms of the universe. Our bodies are designed to work synchronistically. Healthy bodies are locked into the rhythms of perfectly regulated synchronicity. All of our cells have to work in unison with each other and disease happens when some part of our body is out of balance with this naturally occurring synchronicity; the natural rhythm is disrupted.

When we aren't listening to our intuition or taking notice of the synchronicity in our lives, the universe will send us a "wake up call".

A wake up call is a sign that we need to stop and look at our life. There is something that we need to change. It is time to get back in alignment with what it is that is the highest good for ourselves. These calls are giving us the opportunity to begin again, take another route. Do not ignore a wake up call. It is the universe's last resort. Sometimes it takes a drastic action to truly begin living. A wake up call tells us to renew our life and make some modifications – there is something that we need to change; there is something that is not working.

It will put us on the path toward the process of transformation. It will move us in a different direction. It gives us an opportunity to address something or reconsider a certain direction. Divine source is always making attempts to keep us moving in the direction of our soul's journey.

Meditation

Meditation is the stillness of the physical, mental and emotional states that allow the awareness of our energy, our spirit to be felt and acknowledged. When we meditate we still the mind. We close down the superficial ego perception and acknowledge our inner nature. When we close our eyes we remove ourselves from the objective mind, and when we quiet the senses we reacquaint ourselves with the inner voice of truth. Meditation is a great way to free our minds of the world around us. Meditation is the practise of turning inwards to the spirit force that lies within. Meditation offers us the closest experience we can have of reconnecting with our source and being one with the universal intelligence within. When we meditate we transcend the ego and quiet the mind. We can come to know the peace of spirit and we can listen intuitively to spirit's powerful yet silent guidance.

Be still and know that I AM GOD.

> To the mind that is still the whole universe surrenders.
>
> Lao Tzu

Ego cannot survive in the stillness of meditation because when we are in a quiet state, a state of inner peace, we are much more aware and able to listen to our spirit. It is only when we truly become connected to spirit that we start to resonate with it. It is in this realm of stillness that we are able to fully connect to, and develop a deeper understanding of spirit. We can gain the unlimited power of reconnecting with our source through meditation and it will deliver an awareness of the truth of who we really are, and eventually we begin to think like spirit – like one universal mind. This is spiritual intuition.

> Silence is a source of great strength.
>
> Lao Tzu

Meditation is returning to the place where time does not exist and to the place where all of the answers lie. Meditation allows us to reach the level of the soul by easing past the tangle of thoughts and emotions that keep our attention bound to the physical world. When we transcend the ego we move beyond the limitations that harness us to the events and outcomes in the physical world.

> Become totally empty. Quiet the restlessness of the mind. Only then will you witness everything unfolding from emptiness.
>
> Lao Tzu

Reincarnation

Ego believes death is final and that consciousness ceases upon death.

This is one of the greatest misconceptions we have about death – that it is an ending. Death is the conclusion of a specific phase of a soul's journey, and the beginning of the next. It is simply another phase of transition in the spiritual evolutionary pathway of our soul's ongoing existence. It is a quest for growth, lived temporarily on another realm. If we think in terms of a novel, it would be the next chapter. It is that the soul has changed its energy or appearance. The soul has completed its mission in this body, in this lifetime; in this realm. The soul is not born, neither does it die. The soul has no beginning and no end. It just has collective experiences. It is our ongoing journey of evolution.

> It gives me a deep comforting sense that things seen are temporal and things unseen are eternal.
>
> Helen Keller

We are on an endless journey through eternity. We will have lifetime after lifetime. What we don't get done or work out in this lifetime, we will work out in another. There is no death. Our soul can never be taken from us because it is the part of us that is eternal. It is the part of us that lives on forever. All the people who have left this planet will live on in spirit in another realm. And when we leave our physical bodies we will return to spirit. There is no loss, there is no death, just a recycling of energies – a change of form. Spirit knows that physical death is simply a change of state, that consciousness is eternal and as such survives physical death. Spirit welcomes physical death because it knows existence is the never-ending evolution of consciousness and that "death" is a return to a more authentic state of consciousness.

> What the butterfly calls "the end" the rest of the world calls a butterfly.
>
> Lao Tzu

Returning is the motion of spirit. We all come from one universal source and we all return to that one universal source. Everything that exists in this world of form came from something that is formless. Our physical bodies are just an illusion. We don't have to encounter death to feel our unique free spirit. When we are able to return to that place from which we came from and live our lives from a spirit perspective, free from ego, we will experience enlightenment. Love survives death. Love lives on and never dies. Death is just part of the cosmic drama.

When we connect to spirit and live as one with divine love we will know that there is nothing but unconditional love and light. This is what we call home.

> We shall not cease from exploration, and at the end of all our exploring we will return to the place from which we originate and know it for the first time.
>
> T S Elliot

As spiritual beings, we chose to come back to this earth at this time to encounter all of the opportunities that will lead us and the human race forward in the universe's evolution. When we decided to reincarnate again we chose to take on all the responsibilities of life. We come here with a constant knowing and divine guidance and the power to create with our own thoughts and ideas. The mighty secret that has eluded us for centuries is that of remembering our divine nature. All of the power and knowledge that we will ever need is inside us all. All of the answers that we seek to know are inside our own hearts. Without the knowledge that we are spiritual beings having a human experience we remain in the denial of truth. We become victims of circumstance rather than creators of our own lives.

When we choose to reincarnate on earth we bring with us a blueprint of all that has gone before – our past lives and our soul's challenges and lessons.

When we take on human form we release the memories of our prior life experiences in order to start again with a clear conscience. This is all part of the grand plan. By starting over each lifetime afresh, we are free to choose the reality that we want to experience rather than deliberating over decisions made in previous lifetimes. By our choosing the people and situations with which we experience our lives, we bring about our own soul's growth. Only in the material world can we find the opportunities to learn our lessons and have immediate responses to the mistakes that we make along the way which enable us to make a different choice. We are spiritual beings encapsulated in a human form. A soul's greatest regret is getting back to the spirit world not having discovered that they were spirits living a human existence. When we know this for sure we have the power to believe in ourselves; we can choose not to merely exist but to be fully conscious and aware of living in a limited body. We take on a whole new understanding of our role and the universe and when we take a conscious part in our lives and responsibility for the multitude of choices we won't let life happen "to" us – we will make life happen "for" us.

We can see the principles of reincarnation in the universal law of rhythm. We see it in the cycle of nature, day and night, the cyclic motion of the sun, earth, moon and solar system. We also see the principles of reincarnation reflected around us each day; a plant grows and dies, then releases it seeds. Its seeds burrow into the earth, begin to sprout, and new life is reborn once again.

Spring comes and the grass grows by itself.

Lao Tzu

Reincarnation or the rebirth of energy, or life, occurs all around us in different shapes and forms every day. Perhaps this is why to many of us reincarnation resonates the very essence or nature of life. We also see that our lives, and everything around us follows a fundamental pattern; that of change, growth, transformation and evolution. We see that all of life goes through a maturing process at different rates and different times. Thus to many of us, that maturation process of the soul through the progress of reincarnation sounds just as instinctively correct as any other maturing process in life.

Death is an intimate part of life. When we look at the life of plants we notice that every winter the plant dies in order to be reborn into a new season. Some plants live longer than others and it is the same for human beings. It is just a matter of recycling.

Matter cannot be created or destroyed. Everything that dies is just changing into a different material form. The material form itself is composed of energy. We are all pure recycled energy. As the physical body decomposes, the essence of life leaves and returns to the spirit world.

> This quiet dust was ladies and gentlemen
> And lads and girls
> Was laughter and ability and sighing
> And frocks and curls
>
> This passive place a summer's nimble mansion
> Where blooms and bees
> Fulfilled their oriental circuit
> Then ceased like these.
>
> Emily Dickinson

Everything is always on a journey to somewhere else. Everything is on a continuous cycle and will end up back where it came from. Even a drop of rain from the clouds eventually ends up back where it came from. Raindrops fall, filling up the lakes, river and streams. Some of this water is used for human consumption and some is used to tend to our food sources. Eventually though all of the water goes back into the system for recycling. It is evaporated and goes back into the sky to fall as rain again – and so the cycle begins again.

Just like the water, we human beings are just passing through. Everything in the universe is constantly moving and change is inevitable. We are constantly evolving and advancing on our journey. Throughout each of our lifetimes we will experience and absorb all of our memories and emotions and they will contribute greatly to our experiences as we live our lives. Just like the raindrop we will eventually journey back to where we originated from – the spirit world. Only then can we be reborn again to return to this human form. Our soul is eternal as it has no birth and never dies. It continues to exist long after the physical body experiences death, just as it did before entering the earthly realm. When we leave this world we embark on a journey as we return to the spirit world, our natural home, and we arrive in soul form – in perfect health. Our soul does not have an ending; our lives are continuous. Every decision we ever make is vital to our soul's journey. Divine intelligence will continue to guide us in the direction of learning, evolving and thriving. When we trust in the divine guidance and acknowledge the wisdom that is showing and guiding us in our life we will inevitably begin to notice people, synchronicity and intuition helping us along the way. The soul is continually attracting the conditions that it needs in order to evolve. We reincarnate over and over again to help with the progression, evolution and advancement of our souls. With each lifetime the soul continues to grow, learn, transform and evolve as we become more spiritually aware and grow closer to our divine source. We are the total accumulation of all of our learning through different lifetimes, and these experiences create the history of our souls. An unlearned lesson will continue to show up in the next lifetime until we eventually learn the lesson. The education and progression of the soul does not end when we die – it continues to evolve – forever. When we leave the world and begin our next life we continue where we left off, on a higher spiritual plane.

Souls on the other side rejoice and welcome us with open arms when we leave the physical world, just as souls in physical form welcome us with open arms when we arrive in the form of a baby.

When we pass over, we leave this physical plane and enter a higher dimension that vibrates at an elevated frequency and that is why we cannot see it.

When we can accept the fact that we have all had past lives and that we have chosen to come back in order to gain more knowledge and complete the life lessons that we hadn't managed to accomplish in previous lives, our current lives automatically become more meaningful. When we realise that we have selected our own personal lessons as well as our finite time here in human form we will know that we have also chosen our time to pass back into the spirit realm. Because of this we become grateful for our lives and we cease to take our time here for granted. We will cease to maintain a meaningless existence and we will begin to live life more fully.

No weapon can pierce the soul; no fire can burn it; nor water can moisten it; nor can wind wither it.

The self is never born, nor does it ever perish; nor having come into existence will it again cease to be. It is birth-less, eternal, changeless, ever the same, unaffected by the usual processes associated with time.

Bhagavad Gita

Chapter Seven
ENLIGHTENMENT

To become learned each day add something; to become
enlightened each day drop something.

Lao Tzu

We all experience this relentless drive toward unity. It exists within all of
us, no matter how deep in ego we are. There is always a deep longing to
find home and once again be the free spirit we know ourselves to be. It
is an intrinsic part of our existence. The meaning of our lives is to reveal
the beauty of our spirit and embark on a journey of self discovery and
transformation. It is a yearning to know oneself and to awaken to all of
oneself. It is a yearning for answers and direction, for peace, happiness
and eternal love. Evolution is leading us gradually towards higher
consciousness. Every human has an instinct or drive towards spiritual
wholeness. This inner drive constantly pushes us toward fulfilling our
truest self. Spirituality is a personal quest for truth and reality. Our life
is based on a journey – a journey away from ego, and back to spirit; back
to home.

The key to growth is the introduction of higher dimensions
of consciousness into our awareness.

Lao Tzu

The world is not a physical place – it is a state of mind. There is a
power much greater than all of us that is beyond the physical and we have
the power to connect to this source.

When we open our minds to the reality that a divine intelligence is arranging all the pieces of our life, we will discover that this divine force is really nothing more than pure unconditional love. This love is boundless and infinite, and when we think and behave in ways that correspond to this divine love, that is when we will experience the miracles in life.

We all come from and ultimately return to the same realm of consciousness. We all emanate from the one source therefore we are all united. The divine intelligence that we all come from is the whole world of consciousness, therefore we all carry this divine energy inside all of us and we never lose this link. We are ALL divine intelligence. Some of us carry a little more light than others but ultimately we all carry the light. We are all made of pure spirit.

> You are not a drop in the ocean
> You are the entire ocean in a drop.
>
> Rumi

The pure spirit enters our bodies when we are born into our physical selves and leaves when the physical body dies, continuing on in the realm of pure consciousness. The spirit is a frequency of light and so can never die. The light is the frequency of unconditional love. That is all that divine intelligence consists of and when we are filled with the light we then become enlightened.

When humanity raises its level of consciousness and begins to wake up to the light and we finally realise and know that we are all a part of the universal mind our lives will change. We are all one unified human race and we all live on one unified living planet. When we we stop taking the world and each other for granted, and start living from the light – from unconditional love as opposed to fear, our world will change.

Love is the most powerful weapon on the face of the earth.

The source of unconditional love is spirit; the source of our being therefore is within all of us. Unconditional love comes through to us at a soul level, beginning at the level of self acceptance and self forgiveness, and radiates divine light to everyone and everything. When we make a conscious decision to choose thoughts based on unconditional love, it means that we consciously commit ourselves to expressing respect, kindness, and co-operation to everyone and everything in our lives. Unconditional love is the life force of energy within our very being and is ingrained in every cell of our bodies. We don't have to search for love – we ARE, each one of us, the physical embodiment of unconditional love. Because unconditional love is life energy, it is formless, infinite, constantly in motion, and unconditionally available to us. Unconditional love has a positive effect on our physical, emotional, mental, and spiritual state of being, creating truth, joy, beauty, health, harmony, and everything in the world that is in our greatest good. The compassionate nature of universal love flows through us and blesses everyone and everything it touches. When we open our hearts to receiving and expressing the love of the universe, we feel joyous and radiant. We feel fulfilled and whole. We automatically rise above the limitations of fear because unconditional love is infinitely more powerful than fear; in fact, unconditional love is the most powerful force in existence. There is no amount of darkness that can erase light; but the tiniest amount of light can overcome darkness. This means that no matter how dark and chaotic our ego may seem at times, we can find comfort in knowing that our earthly world is always held within an infinitely larger context of universal love and light. Remembering that we are each created in the energy of divine love gives us great inspiration and renewed hope that we each have the power to bring our own unique expression of unconditional love to the world, which brings healing to everyone and everything we touch.

When we stop seeing our lives as separate from all things – separate from others, separate from the world, separate from spirit, separate from the universe and most of all separate from ourselves – we will begin to evolve in limitless ways.

When we know that we are never alone – we are connected to everybody – we will become compassionate and the fighting will cease. We will cease to fight for we will realise that we all are a part of the world. We are all one. We would then come together as fellow human beings and bond. We would create love and friendship, a joining, a sense of caring, belonging and togetherness.

The greed would cease to exist and we would begin to live a united life, when we realised there is more than enough for everybody and we began to share. We would learn to share our valuable resources with each other, then see the war and fighting stop. Greed would be replaced by an attitude of sharing and compassion for and among all. Instead of trying to persecute others we would understand, forgive and tolerate each other.

Destructive and cruel wars are caused by hatred, greed and desire for power, dominance and revenge – all traits of the ego which when transcended, are replaced with unconditional love – the frequency of divine intelligence.

When we open ourselves up and change our mind to, "How may I serve?" (spirit's interpretation) as opposed to, "What's in it for me?" (ego's interpretation) there would be no more starving children.

We will stop competing with each other and comparing ourselves with each other and the bullying will stop.

We will know that to forgive is to free ourselves, therefore there will be a great reduction in the amount of resentment filled cancers. Resentment would disappear with forgiveness and cancer will diminish. Anger will disappear when we realise that all anger stems from fear and hurt and compassion for ourselves and others will resume. We will forgive ourselves for our past mistakes, stop the self criticism and accept ourselves as who we are and we will find that when we make peace and accept ourselves for who we are, life will become so much more enjoyable.

We will become grateful for what we have in our lives as opposed to what we do not, therefore creating more joy and happiness. When we eliminate fear from our lives and replace it with unconditional love we will feel a deep gratitude for everything.

When we realise that material possessions and physical makeup are not important we will learn to experience joy in our lives. When we know that physical appearance is not who we are and that we do not have to conform to society's ridiculous expectations of appearances in order to feel accepted, our lives will take on a whole new meaning. Our priorities will change and we will stop being so harsh on ourselves. Bullying would cease to exist and eating disorders would diminish as we realise that who we are is much more than our physical bodies.

The distrust will stop and we will find freedom and joy once more. When we know that everything that happens is for a reason and everything serves a purpose in our lives we will begin to trust in the process of life and stop blaming ourselves and others for the misfortunes that happen to us. When we know that the universal intelligence is working for us we can let go and let God.

We will realise that worrying about time is a waste of time – guilt over the past and worry over the future is pointless – so we will begin to live in the now and create a lot less stress and tension for ourselves.

We will create peace on earth when we can accept things as they are without judgment.

We will know that whatever we believe we can achieve, so our priorities will change and we will all end up leading more rewarding lives. We will know that when we change our thoughts we will change our lives and when nothing has any meaning except the meaning that we give to it we empower our own lives. When we know that we create our own reality we will stop being a victim and begin by taking an active role in our own lives. When we realise the power of our own minds we will start creating our own lives as never before imagined.

We will know that we are here to have the best experience that we possibly can. We are here to live and to grow and to remember who we are. Our priorities will change as our sense of purpose becomes clearer. Our lives will become richer with a deeper sense of meaning and unconditional love will push out the fear. Having the knowledge that we are all here for a purpose and we are all interconnected will give us a sense of security. We will live for each precious moment and see less sickness, stress related illness such as heart attacks, strokes and stomach ulcers.

We will lose our fear and inhibitions and know that we can achieve whatever we want to in life. We can have faith that when we chase our dreams we can make them come true. We are not limited by fear (ego) or our five senses.

When we transcend the ego we will lose the concept that we are separate from all that there is – separate from others, separate from the universe, separate from spirit and mostly separate from ourselves. When we realise that we all come from the same source and we are all part of the whole, we will realise the damage we are doing to nature. We are causing global devastation which is causing extinction of many animal species. We are losing our pollinators – our birds and bees – as a result of rampant worldwide pesticide use. We know that when we lose the pollinators we will lose much of our much-loved fruit and vegetables. When we can clearly see the knock-on effect of our actions and learn to love the planet we live on and develop a real sense of connection with nature we will stop destroying it with our thoughts and actions.

We will know that everybody has a different opinion and we are given free will so there really is no right or wrong, there is just a perspective, therefore the fighting and arrogance will stop. We will feel the need to stop being so defensive when we know that everybody makes mistakes and that is the way that we are supposed to learn our lessons.

We will begin to see the divine guidance speaking to us in the form of intuition and synchronicity and pay attention to these valuable messages.

With the loss of ego we will learn to love ourselves and therefore self hatred, blame, lack of self confidence and self worth will disappear. Self love will help us turn from compulsive consumers used to filling the void in our hearts where love should have been, into a whole and healed human being displaying joy and inner peace. The anger, pain, anxiety and emptiness that we feel within and try to fill up with external possessions will be replaced with confidence, happiness, fulfillment and delight. Addictions will become healed when we learn to love ourselves unconditionally.

We will realise that ego is responsible for the relentless self judgment, constant self criticism and lack of love and acceptance that is behind every pain, illness, unhappiness or disease and we will grow healthier when we begin to love ourselves and look after our bodies. When we learn to love ourselves our whole experience of life will change and we will experience sheer joy and happiness in ways we have never known.

> Few will have the greatness to bend history itself; but each of us can work to change a small portion of events, and in the total; all of these acts will be written on the history of this generation.
>
> Robert Kennedy

> Imagine no possessions
> I wonder if you can
> No need for greed or hunger
> A brotherhood of man
> Imagine all the people
> Sharing all the world....
>
> John Lennon: Imagine

The deeper our appreciation the more we see with the eyes of the soul and the more our life flows in harmony with spirit.

Our soul knows all that it needs to know. Upon entering this visible world of form, we relinquished our memories of before. This allowed us to choose who we wanted to be. Our soul's purpose is to remember who we are. Remembrance is when we return to spirit.

Enlightenment is experiencing oneness with the universe. We realise that we have finally arrived at that place for which we have been searching for so long.

Seeing the light has finally set us free. It is an understanding of how the universe works. It is knowing that everything in the universe is created from, and is part of the same energy, and knowing in what way we relate to it all. Once we are aware of this, everything makes sense; we see the world with an immense clarity. Everything is understood and our life is suddenly filled with a feeling of immense joy, peace and fulfillment. We find that our communication with the universe becomes effortless.

When we live in spirit we know that we were all created from one divine intelligence. This divine intelligence is within each and every one of us. This is the invisible force that is growing our fingernails, beating our hearts and turning seeds into vegetables.

We realise the fundamental truth in the expression "Everything happens for a reason". The universe comes from a place of purpose therefore we know that every experience that happens to us is always the best possible outcome. We may not be able to identify with the reason but we know that it will be revealed to us at some stage in our lives.

We know that our physical body is not who we are. We stop looking externally for the answers and begin to look within. Enlightenment is not a process of acquiring more knowledge, but is about removing the internal blockages to reveal the light within. Who we are is the light within. Our life before we became an embodiment of spirit was the same as our source and we chose to enter this world of form. When we were in spirit we knew what we were coming here to accomplish. We chose our path and our destination, and then we chose to set this life process into motion. Deep within all of us is an awareness of what our lives are destined to become. When we come to the conclusion that our life plans were created long ago, we can stop blaming other people and other circumstances for the misfortunes that show up in our lives and see them for what they really are. Everything is a part of our own personal life journey and when we look at it from a spiritual perspective, we can see that all of the pieces fit together perfectly. When we realise that we are responsible for everything that we are attracting into our lives, we can eliminate any negative energy. We know that our lives are being lived on purpose. All of the positive and negative situations and events that happen in our lives are part of the plan to bring us closer to our life purpose and that will always be in service to others. Our life's purpose will always be to teach or help somebody else through the lessons we have learned or share the purpose that has been the fundamental truth of our life.

The calling of our divine spirit is, "How may I serve?"

We all come to this earth to remember who we are, to learn from our experiences and to serve. This is our soul's purpose.

Enlightenment is the goal from total amnesia to remembrance. Every one of us will take a different journey to find the way but while there are an infinite number of roads on the journey to enlightenment, none of them change the final destination. When we find the truth we will find peace. The way that we know it is the truth is that it will resonate with us. It will make sense, logically, intellectually, and emotionally. The answers to all of the questions that we have been seeking will have been answered. All of the pieces of the puzzle will finally fit together and we will be able to see with such clarity the meaning of our lives and the way of the universe. Our confusion will banish. Finding the truth we will feel liberated, empowered, clear and whole. And then we will begin to see evidence of the truth everywhere. We will begin to live our lives with a new sense of "knowing" and joy. We will find a happiness that we have been searching for our whole lives. Nothing frees us like the truth and nothing holds us back like not knowing it. Knowledge is power. It heals what is hurt, it fills what is empty, it clears and refreshes what is confused and lightens burdens that are heavy.

The path to our new beginning starts within us all.

> If light is in your heart
> you will find your way home.
>
> Rumi

There in no substitute for spiritual enlightenment. Once we have experienced that enlightening moment of total vision about the true nature of ourselves, our universe and our purpose in the world, our lives will take on a whole new meaning. We will acquire a freedom which is naturally filled with wisdom and compassion. This new connection will give us a new lease on life and a better understanding of ourselves and the world in general. We will evoke a whole new attitude for the meaning of our lives and for living our lives.

> In the end the treasure of life is missed by those who hold
> on, and gained by those who let go.
>
> Lao Tzu

Enlightenment is fundamentally the annihilation of the ego. Transcending the ego moves us closer to enlightenment.

Having this knowledge lets us release the grip that fear (ego) has over us. Knowledge is power and awareness is truth. When we know the truth we can rise to our life ambition; to learn and evolve. When we know the truth all of the judgments, misery and suffering and all the negativity that ego brings into our lives, suddenly disappears. We begin to have a new lease on life and a better understanding of ourselves and the world in general. It gives us a whole new attitude toward living our lives. We are led to a calm, content peace of mind that knows that the universe is under the care of a power much greater than all of us, so we can trust in that. We can let go and let God.

> Imagine if you told a family living in abject poverty that there was a treasure of gold under the dirt floor of their shanty. They would only need to remove the layers of dirt hiding it and they would be rich forever. In the same way, we are not aware of our spiritual nature, hidden by our own ignorance and delusion.
>
> Buddha

Chapter eight
HAPPINESS

We all have a deep and profound desire to find happiness – it is the essence of every one of us – it is our calling. It is that from which we came; it is home. To feel like we did when were one with divine intelligence we will be happy, joyful, fulfilled, grateful and connected. We can relax knowing that we are all safe. We are all loved unconditionally.

> The snow goose need not bathe to make itself white
> Neither need you do anything but be yourself.
>
> Lao Tzu

We attract into our lives that which we focus on. We can see the results of our most dominant thoughts by how we are living our lives in the present moment. Our successes will depend on what we perceive them to be; how much money we have accumulated, the possessions that we own, the state of our health or our enjoyment of life. Our spirit is always guiding us toward a life full of happiness and contentment. It is what we came from; it is that deep desire that is within us all.

> Let yourself be silently drawn by the strange pull of what
> you really love. It will not lead you astray.
>
> Rumi

Life is meant to be enjoyable and fulfilling. When we begin to make decisions based on what makes us happy, peaceful and joyful, our lives will begin to have more meaning and pleasure.

No man is a failure who is enjoying life.

William Feather

It is possible to have a life that we truly love, filled with enthusiasm, love and abundance. If we commit to making decisions from the perspective of joy, we will begin to live a life that is truly blessed.

From experience we know that when we feel fear, we are not feeling in a good state of mind. Experience also tells us that there is a certain state of mind that we are in when we feel love. True happiness is not just an emotion but a state of being; therefore happiness is a state of mind.

To be or not to be.

Shakespeare

Rather than looking externally for the things we think will create happiness we need to go within and explore our core selves.

Happiness requires that we let go of all the attributes we associate with ego – fear, hatred, selfishness, anger, jealousy, obsession and dishonesty and begin living with the positive attributes that we associate with spirit – love, peace, harmony, joy, fulfillment, honesty, inner strength, confidence and serenity.

Everything already exists with us. We are all the same. We are all inseparable from all that exists. Because we are all an extension of divine intelligence, and divine intelligence is the source of all reality, then we are the source of all reality. We create our own experience. We all want to be happy and to be fulfilled. We all want meaning and purpose in our lives. We all want a sense of connection to our spirit. We want others to love and respect us and we want to feel safe. These desires are universal. But the journey that each one of us takes to fulfill these desires is uniquely our own, based on our own individual experiences. Fundamentally we are all seeking the same things.

Life itself is the great journey. There is no destination. Our happiness depends on us understanding this. Each moment of every day is a part of this journey and every moment has the potential to fulfill us and make us happy. All of our experiences, events and situations are opportunities we have as individuals to create memorable moments in our life's journey and within the meaning of each of these simple activities lies the meaning of our lives. Whatever we are experiencing at any given moment is an opportunity to experience gratitude, joy and compassion and in doing so will create the eternal path to happiness.

> Remind yourself daily – there is no way to happiness; happiness is the way.
>
> Lao Tzu

We are each put here for a specific purpose. A basic need of all human beings is to make a positive contribution toward the world and our fellow beings as well as to improve and enjoy our personal lives. We all have a gift to offer the world and each other in our own special and unique way. Whatever our life's purpose, it will involve making a significant contribution to something or somebody. To a degree, our own personal sense of well-being is a function of how well we are expressing this. Enlightenment is knowing what our higher purpose is. It is being our total authentic self and once we discover our life's purpose, we will feel whole and true to ourselves. It is a knowing that we are fulfilling our destiny.

> Happiness cannot be travelled to, owned, earned, worn or consumed. Happiness is the spiritual experience of living every moment with love, grace and gratitude.
>
> Denis Waitley

Happiness is not created as a result of certain conditions. Certain conditions are created as a result of happiness. Happiness comes from our own perception; therefore happiness is a choice. True happiness can be obtained by accepting things as the way they are, as opposed to how we think they SHOULD be. Happiness is a decision as opposed to a sudden occurrence that happens as a consequence of ongoing pursuit. Pursuing happiness in itself is a fear based action – we are afraid of not achieving the level of happiness that we require. We fight against the universal laws. When we listen to spirit we remember that in the pure conscious state we are all universal energy. Happiness is available to all of us.

If you learn only one thing in this lifetime, let it be this:
You are responsible for creating your own happiness.

Bartholmew

The key to happiness is to stop pursuing it and to realise that it already exists within each and every one of us. We just have to allow it to be. Allowing happiness requires no effort; allowing happiness is a state of mind.

Letting go of ego, learning to ground ourselves in the "here" and "now," and turning inwards to the deepest-most-inner-depths of our soul, will ultimately lead to inner peace, and provide a great sense of worth. What a great revelation it is to know that the happiness we have been searching for, for such a long time, is already within us. When we start appreciating everything in life, even the moments that we think are insignificant and we don't take anything for granted, we will discover our own spirit that lies within, and the secret to our happiness will have been revealed.

Self love

We are all here to learn certain life lessons, but the most important lesson to learn is how to love and accept ourselves just as we are.

Happiness begins with loving and accepting ourselves unconditionally.

Self love is a positive heart-centered feeling, radiating warmth and joy within ourselves and out into the world, encompassing everything in a joyful spirit. Our path to self love is also a part of our journey to life satisfaction and happiness.

As love is the most noble and divine passion of the soul,
so it is that to which we may justly attribute all the real
satisfactions of life, and without it, man is unfinished and
unhappy.

Aphra Behn

Learning to love ourselves is the only way to obtain true happiness. Happiness occurs only when we love ourselves. Happiness is apparent when our lives are lived from an attitude of unconditional love, towards ourselves, others and the entire universe. The level of self love that we have for ourselves will determine the amount of happiness we have in our lives.

Happiness and self love are choices. The universe can only work its magic when we are loving and accepting of ourselves.

When we let the ego take over and believe what it tells us we can liken that experience to yelling and screaming at a small child; telling that child that it is stupid, worthless and unloveable. We end up with a very afraid, unhappy little child that has no self worth or joy in its life. Essentially that is what we are doing to ourselves when we let the ego take over. The ego lives in shame, unworthiness and guilt. It tells us that we are not good enough and we are not worthy. When we live with resentment, guilt, fear and criticism of ourselves we create diseases that destroy the body. Fear is not trusting in the process of life. When we do not love and accept ourselves it means that were are still believing the old limiting beliefs that our egos took on a long time ago. Spirit guides us to change those limiting beliefs – when we change our thoughts we change our lives.

The goal in this physical world is to learn to love ourselves for who and what we are as spiritual and human beings. Our goal and main priority is to figure out and discover who we really are and to learn to extend unconditional love unto ourselves. When we fail to find unconditional love and acceptance for ourselves we feel disappointed and frustrated about our lives. There appears to be something missing that is necessary to provide happiness in our lives – and that is self acceptance. We need to lose the labels and false opinions of others that we have been carrying around in our subconscious and learn to love ourselves unconditionally for who and what we are before true happiness can ever happen.

When we live our life in spirit we allow ourselves to embrace that inner child and tell it that it is loved, it is worthy and it is clever and beautiful. It is alright to make mistakes and no matter what the circumstance, we will always be there for that child. When we were children all we wanted was love and approval and to some extend we are all still looking for that love and approval, but other people's approval means nothing unless we give it to ourselves. When we can accept ourselves without judgment and criticism we allow freedom and joy to re-enter our lives.

When we live our lives in spirit we stop all the criticism. We approve of ourselves and we accept ourselves. Love is the healing power. Love dissolves anger. Love removes guilt. Love overcomes fear. Love for ourselves is the power that heals us. No negative condition can exist in our lives when we truly love and accept ourselves. Love for thyself detoxifies the ego.

Self acceptance is the reflection which determines how we perceive the experiences, events and situations in our lives. Our self image determines our perception of success or failure, our thoughts about ourselves and other people's reaction to us. Our self image determines our focus and what we allow ourselves to think about. Our reaction to the experiences, events and situations that occur in our lives is what determines our happiness. To reach a higher consciousness we need to change the concept we have about ourselves.

When we love and accept ourselves unconditionally, we will love and accept the world just as it is. We are exactly what we believe ourselves to be. We can take responsibility for being the deciding factor of our own self image. We choose our own self worth and decide how much happiness we will allow into our lives. When we love and approve of ourselves exactly as we are, then life begins to flow and our whole world changes.

> One does not walk into the forest and accuse the trees of being off centre, nor do we visit the shores and call the waves imperfect. So why do we look at ourselves this way?
> Tao Te Ching

Self approval and self acceptance in the now are the ways in which we detach from the ego. Health, love and wholeness cannot survive where there is constant self judgment. All of the happiness, love and peace cannot occur without us having self love and acceptance. The more we detach from the ego, the more the spirit replaces the ego and ego begins to diminish and then we have more potential to experience love and peace.

Ego insists on diminishing self esteem and thrives on lack of self esteem.

To harness the power of self esteem, we need to take responsibility for the fact that we have free will and we can either listen to the negative perspective of the ego or know that we can identify with spirit – who we really are. Self acceptance happens when we realise that we are spiritual beings who are free from limitations and know that we can trust that divine love and guidance is available at every moment.

Just because we are human beings, we are inherently unique and special. Being unique is our value and our value is our contribution to this universe. We are all unique in the fact that we were all given gifts to use as part of our earthly journey. Everybody is given different gifts and when we all come together and use our universal gifts in a united position, we can then create and experience some truly wonderful lifetimes. From this perspective we all have a sacred and obligatory contribution to make while here on this earth. Understanding this gives greater clarification to the illusion that we are all separate. Spirit wants nothing more than for us to awaken from the illusion that we are all separate. When we can all use our gifts and work together, we can change the world.

At the higher end of our soul's frequency is our spirit self. This connects us directly to the spiritual realms and transcends our limited consciousness. The spirit self is one of joy, love, compassion and happiness. The spirit self contains the uncontaminated and pure elements of our soul that are waiting to be discovered and expressed. Whenever we feel these emotions we are coming from our natural state; our "spirit self".

At the lower end of our soul's frequency is our false self, our ego self. It is completely focused on itself and is completely at the mercy of the illusions of the physical world. It is completely identified with fear and external commodities and is the cause of our ongoing unhappiness, resentment, guilt and lack of love.

When we are able to move beyond the lowly desires of the ego self and become aware of the higher elements of our true being we will discover happiness. We must remember that first and foremost we are already spirit; spirit already exists.

When we discover that who we are is an integral part of spirit, how can we not begin to love ourselves? Spirit is a state of being and spirit is within each and every one of us and spirit is made from love. Therefore love is completely surrounding us at all times. Love can free us from all darkness (ego). It is always available, within our reach and in complete abundance for us all. Love is all there is. Finding and reconnecting to love once again is fundamentally the most important thing we as humans beings can do for the evolution of our universe. Spirit is unconditional love and we are part of spirit. Therefore we are spirit and thus we are unconditional love. Loving ourselves and others unconditionally is the reason for our existence and it is the answer to a happy, fulfilled and joyous life.

It is our egos that are not allowing ourselves to feel that love. Ego is the obstacle of our entitled birthright. When we do not allow love to embrace our lives, we are denying the spirit within, expressing itself through us.

When we allow ourselves to be loved and accepted unconditionally in the present moment, we will find that our lives acquire a much more meaningful and enjoyable expression. When we cultivate a loving and positive relationship with ourselves, we can know the miracle of self love and the freedom and abundance of joy that it will bring to our lives.

Happiness and joy is ultimately self love and self acceptance. It is freedom from self judgment and criticism. It is freedom from ego. When we have reached the place of transcending the ego we can live without fear and then become a free spirit.

> If you knew who walked beside you at all times, on the path that you have chosen, you could never experience fear or doubt again.
>
> Wayne Dyer

Printed in the United States
By Bookmasters